The Daily Telegraph

STARTING & RUNNING A B&B

·REVISED AND UPDATED· SECOND EDITION· **2**

A practical guide to setting up and managing a successful Bed & Breakfast business

STEWART WHYTE

howtobooks

Published by How To Books Ltd
Spring Hill House, Spring Hill Road
Begbroke, Oxford OX5 1RX
Tel: (01865) 375794. Fax: (01865) 379162
info@howtobooks.co.uk
www.howtobooks.co.uk

First edition 2003
Reprinted 2003
Reprinted 2004 (twice)
Reprinted 2005
Second edition 2006

British Library Cataloguing in Publication Data
A catalogue record for this book is available from the British Library

ISBN 13: 978 1 84528 156 4
ISBN 10: 1 84528 156 X

Cover design by Baseline Arts Ltd, Oxford
Produced for How To Books by Deer Park Productions
Illustrations by Nicki Averill
Typeset by PDQ Typesetting, Newcastle-under-Lyme, Staffs.
Printed and bound in Great Britain by Bell & Bain Ltd., Glasgow

Contents

To invite someone to be our guest
Is to undertake responsibility for
Their happiness all the time that
They are under our roof.

Jean Anthelme Brillat-Savarin (1755–1826)
Author, epicure, raconteur

Preface

The growth of Bed & Breakfast as an accommodation alternative is a success story unparalleled throughout the Western world and, in particular, the United Kingdom and Ireland. To meet demand and substantiate Bed & Breakfast's place in the tourism industry there is now a growing need for increased knowledge and professionalism among Bed & Breakfast operators. Far too many are catering for the lower end of the market when more establishments should be providing better facilities and service for the ever-growing numbers of discerning and affluent travellers.

Participation in tourism can be an exciting lifestyle venture, especially in the Bed & Breakfast industry. It is relatively easy to enter and has the potential to be both financially and personally rewarding. The traditional Bed & Breakfast is a privately owned premises that offers value for money, accommodation inclusive of breakfast, quaintness and hospitality, and opportunities for the guest to exchange ideas with the host and be the recipient of sound, local, and sightseeing advice. In the main, the traditional B&B is a home where both the host and their guests are sheltered under the same roof.

The above definition applies to small hotels, some pubs, and guest houses that have no more than eight serviced bedrooms and is current throughout the United Kingdom, Ireland, the Channel Islands and the Isle of Man. The six-bedspace rule may apply.

The conceptional focus, however, is placed on the personal interaction and assistance the host provides to the guest and not just the bricks and mortar content. This is what forms the true intrinsic value of Bed & Breakfast accommodation.

As aside from the interest in entering the market as a proprietor, there is increasing interest by the public in staying in B&Bs while touring, or as a viable short break holiday option. With this rise in popularity, however, come expectations and those are what we discuss in this book.

Current trends show that changes in the workplace could be one of the main contributors to the high level of interest in becoming a B&B operator. Another influential factor is the growth of the short-break holiday market. Those who take short-break holidays historically prefer this form of accommodation.

It is important to remember, however, that knowledge is not an end in itself. You must use the knowledge gained from this publication as a resource and stepping stone to achieve your goals and aspirations. The main message is that the research you need to do to make your B&B a success must be personal to you and your market.

This second edition of *Starting & Running a B&B – A practical guide to setting up and managing a Bed & Breakfast* has been assembled by a team of experienced researchers and operators who have carefully studied the practicalities and the needs of people who are either in the industry or wishing to enter it. In constructing the book we have tried to avoid duplication of material that exists in other training manuals and how-to publications, preferring to concentrate on that which is directly applicable to the industry. We have gathered up-to-date information from industry leaders and practitioners, both nationally and internationally, to give the reader a source of information, which reflects the practicalities and requirements necessary for the successful Bed & Breakfast operator.

There is included in this second edition, two *new* sections devoted to assisting the reader in completing a feasibility study prior to leaping into the B&B business, plus another section showing you how to develop and write your own business plan.

All of these issues are significant, but professionalism is the most important. This book will reinforce the need to seek professional advice in the early stage of your venture and give you an insight into the level of professionalism you need to consider in order to be a success in this business. Good luck on your venture!

Stewart Whyte

Acknowledgements

This book would not be as comprehensive without the wonderful contribution of the following people and organisations:

Paul Ricardo for his Internet advice; Dr Rita Helling for her comments on linguistic programming; Nigel Jess for his initial input, Gideon and Sara Stanley from Gracesoft; Sealy of UK.

Star UK, Northern Ireland Tourist Board, Bord Fáilte, Department of Tourism and Leisure – Isle of Man and Jersey and Guernsey Tourism regarding tourism research statistics, also Abergavenny, Exeter, Windermere, Keswick, Stamford and Worcester Tourist Offices; the Scottish Tourist Offices and Colin Houston from VisitScotland; Wales Tourist Board, for their helpful insights; Northern Ireland Farm & Country Holidays Association, N.I. Bed & Breakfast Association, The Town & Country Homes Association (Bed & Breakfast Ireland), The Irish Farmhouse Holidays Association, (Fáilte Tuaithe), Bed & Breakfast (UK) Ltd, AA Hotel Services – Lifestyle Guides.

Jacqueline Elmslie; Max Mosher and Energy Saving Trust for their advice on energy saving considerations; Warren Whyte, Managing Director UK & Europe of Custom House (Global Foreign Exchange) for his advice on banking procedures.

William Fry, Solicitors Dublin for their respective advice on liquor licensing, The Ryan Insurance Group for their advice on business insurance for B&B operators, Wal Reynolds – co-author of the feasibility study and the business plan sections: this includes material from *Your Own Business*, Reynolds, Savage & Williams, used with permission.

I would also like to thank Jo and Graham Moule of Mount Tavy Cottage Bed & Breakfast, in Tavistock for the photograph used on our front cover.

This book is easy to read due to the editing expertise of Suellen Harwood. Her research skills and ability to expand the text is greatly appreciated. For this I thank her.

I would like to thank all of the Bed & Breakfast owners for their advice and tips which will prove invaluable to all the newcomers in the industry.

Until next time,

Stewart

Introduction

Starting & Running a B&B – A practical guide to setting up and managing a Bed & Breakfast is divided into two main sections for easy access. The first section is designed for you to discover if you, your partner and family, your home and your bank balance are ready to enter this industry. It will also allow you to decide what level of commitment you are prepared to make to this venture: full-time/weekends/breakfasts only/full board, etc. We also show you how to undertake a feasibility study that tests the viability of your commercial proposition before you start spending money and time on it.

If you have decided that operating a Bed & Breakfast is your dream for a better future, then Section Two will be an introduction to the daily issues that confront Bed & Breakfast operators, as it outlines how to run a Bed & Breakfast efficiently and successfully. Included in this section are the guidelines to completing your own business plan.

Throughout this book you will find two symbols. The single symbol 🏠 is applicable to all operators, but in particular to those whose commitment to the enterprise is on a very small scale (perhaps one or two bedrooms, and not the only source of income). The double symbol 🏠 🏠 is for those whose enterprise will run on a larger scale and who need it to contribute substantially to the household income.

The following are a number of questions you might like to ask yourself before you read any further. As you progress through the book you may wish to return to this page to see how your ideas on what it takes to run a successful Bed & Breakfast have altered.

- What parts of my character make me a perfect host or hostess?

- What implications do I think that owning and operating a Bed & Breakfast will have on my personal life?

- Who will be my target market?

- What facilities do I already have?

- What additional facilities do I think I will need to provide or acquire?

- What financial investment do I think will be needed to start the venture?

- Do I have this amount of finance available?

- If not, where do I expect it will come from?

- Who do I expect to be my customers?

- Why will they come to my Bed & Breakfast rather than some other type of accommodation?

- How will my potential customers hear about my Bed & Breakfast?

- Will I advertise? If so, where will I advertise?

- How much do I intend to charge?

- What factors did I look at to reach this figure?

- What factors will influence whether my establishment makes a profit or loss?

- What legal obligations do I have?

- What are the main skills needed to run a successful Bed & Breakfast?

- What are my main skills?

- What kinds of additional help will I require?

- Where will this help come from?

- How much do I know about employing people?

- When do I intend to begin accommodating guests?

- What factors are most likely to inhibit me?

- What will my feasibility study contain and does it make sense?

Having taken stock of your current expectations and knowledge, we will begin looking into the who, what, why and wherefores of operating a successful Bed & Breakfast in the United Kingdom, the Republic of Ireland, the Channel Islands and the Isle of Man.

Part One

Preparing to Enter the B&B Business

1

It's Up To You

S o, you want to run a Bed & Breakfast! *Why?* This is very possibly the most important question you will ask yourself as you read this book.

Why? Is it because you have stayed in a few over the years and it seems such a nice way to earn a living? Is it because you went away for the weekend and saw this gorgeous period or historic homestead and it was only £375,000 or €547,500 and it would be such fun to do up, and hadn't you both talked about making a s*ea change* decision and moving out of the city? Is it because you really like to cook, and have always loved it when your best friend and her family visit you from distant places? Is it because you think it will be a way to make your fortune?

There are many different reasons people enter the Bed & Breakfast market and you need to think clearly about why it is that you wish to enter it. Because, make no mistake about it, the difference between a good and bad B&B is you, the host. Why you are embarking on this adventure matters, because you need to create a business plan that will match the goals you have for your Bed & Breakfast. Be prepared to discover that running a B&B may not achieve those goals for you.

The harsh news first: very few B&Bs will support you in the first few years. First things first: if you start with two guest bedrooms your earning capacity will be limited.

The main reasons for failure are over capitalising on the part of the owners, and the management process of the property itself. Burnout can also be a significant factor in the pursuit of a lifestyle change.

There is a difference in spending on essentials, such as en suites in each guest bedroom, which are rapidly becoming a necessity, and filling your house with expensive antiques which will not always make a guest decide to stay with you, or to return.

A flair for redecorating does not necessarily make you a good host. Neither does enjoying entertaining friends and family. Running a Bed & Breakfast is a 24-hour commitment. You need to be prepared to 'entertain' at all hours of the day and night, have your private life disturbed, and in some cases share your personal space with strangers. This is difficult, but if you are to be a successful host the spirit of giving must be embraced 24 hours a day. This spirit should inhabit every exchange, every phone call, every letter or email. To be a successful host you need to *love people* and be prepared to share your life and home with them. But, never forget quality time for yourself and your family.

IT'S ALL ABOUT PERSONALITY

As you work through this book you are going to be asked a lot of questions. Now is the time to start a notebook to record the answers to all the questions asked of you. This will

be invaluable in determining your market and creating your feasibility study. At the same time start a folder for filing all the information you will need to collect prior to starting your B&B.

◆ Do you have the type of personality that will make you a wonderful host? Write down your answers and refer to them later when evaluating whether you are the right kind of person to run a Bed & Breakfast.

◆ Do you like people? This is very important. You can't just think that people are OK when you enter the B&B industry. You need to genuinely like people and be interested in them. You have to love individuals and the idiosyncrasies that come with individualism.

◆ Are you prepared to do almost anything to make your guests feel important and spoiled? This is the essence of a good host.

◆ Will you enjoy guests, who are in effect strangers, wandering in and out of your home, treating it as if it were their own? When you are living in the same house as your guests, privacy will become a thing of the past.

◆ Are you willing to be available 24 hours a day? Guests and potential guests have the habit of calling, arriving or wanting your help at the most inopportune times. You need to be prepared to drop whatever it is you are doing and provide service with a smile.

◆ Are you going to be able to live with a difficult person over the whole time of their visit? And will you be able to cope with this person in your home? People can be difficult and if you don't have the patience of a saint you may find this life hard.

◆ Can you accept the old adage that the customer is always right? Guests, or potential guests, may be demanding and want things that are unreasonable. Some of their needs will be impossible, however you must be prepared to compromise and try to make your guest happy whenever possible, even when it's against your better judgement. You can't afford to be Basil Fawlty! Word of mouth is the key here, use it as a marketing tool. Your guests' stay should be of such high quality that they act as your ambassadors, spreading the good news of your B&B.

> **TIP**
>
> If you can't find it in your heart to make a grumpy person smile, keep out of the people business.

◆ Are your partner and family as equally committed to this lifestyle choice as you are? Without passion on all sides you may be destined for failure, early burnout, or at worst, relationship difficulties.

◆ Are you a dedicated housekeeper? Untidiness just won't do as a Bed & Breakfast operator. You need to be a fastidious housekeeper. Do you enjoy vacuuming every day? Do you notice if something is out of place? Do your friends call you a perfectionist? Good.

These are the perfect qualities for a B&B host, where near enough is never good enough.

THE DREAM OF WORKING FOR YOURSELF

Being you own boss can be a great way to earn a living. Let's face it, most of us have had this dream. Being able to throw in our job and to go out on our own. Make our mark. Keep the profits for ourselves. And for many that is where it stays – a dream. However, a few of us decide to take the plunge and whether or not we are successful in our endeavour primarily depends on two things: our motivation for entering a business to begin with, and our preparedness for entering that business at that time.

Successful small business operators have chosen to work for themselves for positive reasons. Not because they hate what they are leaving behind, but because they are excited about creating something for the future – including profits. They often are extremely motivated and self disciplined. Not only does your goal need to be uppermost in your mind when opening your own business, you must have the discipline to divide work from your private life – particularly when your business is in your home. Successful small business people thrive away from the constraints of an employer.

Financial goals are also an important focus for the successful small business owner. Your business plan needs to clearly set out the financial goals for your business with strategies to help you reach them. The most successful small business people have a financial and career goal that is unable to be satisfied by working for someone else.

You also need to realise you are leaving the world of the secure pay packet. Gone forever are the hidden financial benefits of working for a wage or salary. It is now all up to you. You need to feel comfortable about this and could consider consulting a financial planner for advice about managing your financial future.

THE FINANCIAL REALITY

The bad news is that most small businesses fail during the first three years. The main reason for this is lack of planning by the owner, both at the set-up stage and ongoing. Entering the ranks for the wrong reason to begin with exacerbates this.

The worst reasons to go into business for yourself are: that no one else will employ you; you want flexible working hours, that is, more time to play than work; and you think that all it takes to make a fortune in your own business is – a good idea. This last statement is the biggest misconception.

The best ideas in the world won't work if you don't plan to succeed – and have the ability to convince everyone else that your idea *is* a good idea. The reasons most often cited for failure in small businesses are:

◆ a lack of business and/or management experience;
◆ inadequate, inaccurate or non-existent financial records;
◆ taking too much money from the business for personal use; and
◆ lack of adequate seed capital.

A solid business plan will help prevent you becoming another statistic. We all know about the bottom line, but the top line, that is, research, is equally important. Thorough research in the early stages of your venture makes you less likely to fail in the long run.

Consider both the advantages and disadvantages of being your own boss.

There is no doubt that it will place some stresses on your lifestyle and relationships in the first few years while you establish a pattern.

Bonuses can be satisfaction, management autonomy and building financial independence. Negatives can be sporadic income, long and irregular hours, competition, possible failure, and relationship difficulties.

MONEY IN THE BANK

Unless you are going into Bed & Breakfast as a hobby or interest, money could be a problem for the first few years.

Many B&B operators make the mistake that holidaymakers are just waiting for them to open their doors and then they will be booked up for months. This doesn't always happen. A significant number of guests will stay at your property based on word of mouth and word of mouth takes time to gather momentum.

You need to have a plan on how you will financially survive until you build a clientele. How much money do you have in the bank? How long can you survive with your outgoings outweighing your income? Do you fully own your property? (This is the most comfortable financial option.) Do you or your partner plan to supplement your income with a second job?

Think about these questions and try to put together a **financial contingency plan** allowing for a slow flow of guests at first.

A LOOK IN THE MIRROR

Before we go any further I want you to look in the mirror. Hard. Then ask yourself the following questions. An *honest* answer to these questions will help you decide whether you are the right person to enter the B&B market and will help to reduce the potential for failure.

- Are you self-driven? When you work for yourself you need to be able to motivate yourself.

- Are you organised? Running a business by yourself or with a partner, needs systematic planning.

- Do both you and your partner share the right temperament to be a B&B host? Are you both friendly, relaxed, organised and charming?

- Are you a problem solver or do you tend to become indecisive when faced with a lot of problems or questions? Running a business requires constant decision-making and the ability to prevent a crisis.

- Are you confident, without being overbearing? You need to be able to sell your business to banks, customers, the media, etc. The essence of a good B&B operator, however, is warmth of personality, you need to have the ability to attract people to you, not distance them from you.

- Are you willing to take advice and learn from others? Successful business people are always on the lookout for good ideas and advice. They then take the best of this and mould it into their business. They work on their business not in it.

- Are you prepared to learn the skills needed to run a business? This takes time and effort.

+ Are you experienced in leading people, and are you prepared to learn? Owning a business often requires you to hire, motivate, and in the worst cases, dismiss staff. This takes a certain skill.

+ Have you the ability to set clear and attainable goals? You need a business plan that is achievable otherwise you are setting yourself up for disappointment.

+ Have you skills of negotiation? Owning your own business will require the forming of relationships with other business people around you. In times of conflict, you need to be able to negotiate win-win agreements with all parties concerned.

+ Can you handle stress? If heavy traffic or queues worry you, this is nothing to the stress you may experience when you have a cash flow problem – an all too common problem when operating a small business.

+ Do you have strong communication skills? Being a host requires the attributes of a perfect personality. You need to be naturally pleasant and agreeable. Those of you who are moody will very likely not find this way of life to your liking. You need to be able to make conversation while avoiding political or religious topics, or other discussion minefields. You need to be patient and tolerant and know the difference between making polite conversation and becoming a nuisance.

A FAMILY AFFAIR

Operating a Bed & Breakfast with a family means that not only should you have the right personality for hosting guests, but so should the other members of your family. Success in

TIP

Before going into the business of Bed & Breakfast stay in a few yourself so as to better understand what the host has to cope with.

Bed & Breakfast is dependent on an equal commitment from everybody concerned. Living on the premises of your business can be distracting enough for an individual – for those of you with a family this disruption can be ten-fold. It is not impossible for you to run both a successful B&B and raise a family on the same premises, but it does require family co-operation and understanding.

You should factor into your business plan contingencies that should ensure the success of your business without disrupting your family's happiness. You might want to consider the following.

Having a defined letting period to protect your family's privacy. For example, you might only let rooms four nights a week or 40 weeks a year, taking your break in the low season. This limitation will, however, affect your income projections, so you must factor this into your feasibility study or business plan.

Consider having a separate annex for your family so that family life is separated from your business life. Organise time out for you and your family to spend time away from your 'office'. No one wants to spend 365 days a year, 24 hours a day at his or her workplace.

If you have children living at home then three nights and four days of having guests may be the maximum – if you want to retain family unity.

Have a friend or colleague who can be available to step in and act as a paid caretaker of your business should you need to get away, or if you are unwell.

Factor in time to discuss and explain to your children why you are entering this business and what the consequences may be for them. Their co-operation will be directly proportional to their level of understanding.

Explain to your children that they are to be polite and friendly to guests at all times, and not to impose on them unless asked. Remember many couples who frequent B&Bs come to escape their children – they won't really want to spend time with yours.

If your children are very young, you should really consider whether now is the right time for you to open your B&B. Both raising very young children and running a B&B are physically and emotionally draining. Trying to juggle both could see you lose your sense of balance.

The other consideration of running a B&B with children at home is that they will want to spend time with you when they are at home, which is primarily at weekends. Weekends, however, are often your busiest trading period. You will need to balance these two claims on your time.

Equal commitment within your family structure is crucial. Tension between family members becomes palpable and your guests will feel it. This will be uncomfortable for all concerned and will not result in return visits.

GOING IT ALONE

Is it possible to do this without a family? It certainly is – more and more Bed & Breakfasts are being run

> **TIP**
>
> Be mindful of the impact Bed & Breakfast has on family life, especially if your children still live at home. Life as you know it will never be the same.

by single people. In some ways you may find this way of life easier than those with a family or an uncommitted partner, as you know you are committed to your business and will ensure that everything is as it should be.

The only disadvantages are time-out periods – which you will need if you are to be successful. Ensure that you have time out from the business to do other things you enjoy. If you have always wanted to do drawing classes, do it. If you want to go on holidays think of hiring an experienced couple to mind your operation while you are away – there are a number of professionals who specialise in this. Have your phone calls linked to your mobile and participate in life.

The other thing is not to over-host your guests – or use them to stave off loneliness. As a good B&B host you should know when your guests want your company and when they do not. This is where your people skills will come in.

IT'S TIME
So you are comfortable that you have the right personality to make a success of the Bed & Breakfast business.

It's now time to get a better appreciation of the tourist trends as they apply to your country. This is important information to know because it can influence future decisions.

TIP

One of the nice things about Bed & Breakfast is the flexibility of being able to decide when to have guests.

2
Who is My Market?

B efore deciding exactly whom you are going to target for your
Bed & Breakfast, it is a good idea to know something about
tourism in your country. The following statistics were obtained
from the following sources:

- Star UK, sponsored by the national tourist boards of England,
  Northern Ireland, Scotland, Wales and the Department for
  Culture, Media and Sport.
- Bord Fáilte – Tourism Facts 2004
- Northern Ireland Tourist Board.

INTERNATIONAL MARKET

Tourism is one of the largest industries in the United Kingdom,
Ireland, the Channel Islands and the Isle of Man. As a guide, I
have listed below in table form, the base 2005 (2005 figures are
provisional) year indicators, which will enable you to better
understand how big your market is.

VisitBritain forecasts an increase in the number of inbound
visitors coming to the UK, for the 2006 year. Growth rates are
expected to further moderate from the sharp increases seen

during 2004 and the early months of 2005. Their inbound forecast for 2006 is as follows:

◆ The volume of inbound tourism to reach 30.6 million visits in 2006, an increase of 4.4% on 2005.

◆ The value of inbound tourism is forecast to grow by 4.3% in 2006 to £14.5 billion.

◆ The strongest growth in 2006 is expected to come from Asia and from emerging markets in Eastern Europe – the slowest growth is expected to come from the Americas.

UK regional distribution

	Visits (000)	Nights (000)	Spend (£m)	Sample size
Total England	25,229	212,929	12,278	37,500
Scotland	2,458	24,991	1,248	2,918
Wales	959	7,208	305	1,231
Northern Ireland	314	1,646	131	181
Irish Republic	2,317	9,217	733	1,748
Isle of Man	12	124	5	21
Channel Islands	16	125	9	27

Accommodation selected

United Kingdom	Visits (000)	Nights (000)	Spend (£m)	Sample size
Hotel/Guest house	11,451	45,291	5,826	18,716
Bed & Breakfast	1,177	8,576	481	1,570
Irish Republic	Visits (000)	Nights (000)	Spend (£m)	Sample size
Hotel/Guest house	822	2,023	297	685
Bed & Breakfast	106	447	35	80

© Crown Copyright: Office for National Statistics 'International Passenger Survey'

England by region

	Visits (000)	Nights (00)	Spend (£m)	Sample size
Total England	25,229	212,929	12,278	37,500
London	13,836	91,075	6,862	23,994
England's North Country	3,813	31,459	1,465	4,243
Central	4,789	40,583	1,633	5,726
Southern	5,880	49,504	2,293	8,972
North East	582	4,997	202	695
North West	2,318	18,038	877	2,482
Yorkshire	1,131	8,424	387	1,375
West Midlands	1,718	13,614	556	1,907
East Midlands	1,101	9,187	378	1,288
East	2,157	17,782	700	2,791
South West	2,090	17,285	831	3,037

© Crown Copyright: Office for National Statistics 'International Passenger Survey'

Wales

In 2004 domestic (UK) staying visitors to Wales accounted for 8.9 million trips, 31.5 million nights and a spend of £1,492 million of which holidays are the most common single purpose (73%). Tourism in Wales shows a traditional 'peak' in June, July and August, which accounts for well over a third of all tourism trips.

Regional distribution within Wales

	Trips/Visits millions	Nights millions	Spending £ millions
North	2.4	12	418
Mid	1.2	6.1	180
South East	1.2	6.1	254
South West	1.3	6.6	260

Scotland

The 2005 audit of tourism accommodation in the City of Glasgow showed that there was a net decline in the guest house and B&B sectors – 122 bed spaces (44% of the total number of operations; 60% of the bed spaces).

The growth in the serviced apartment category (a new category in VisitScotland's QA Scheme) – previously categorised 'self-catering' – from 1 in 2001 to 450 bed spaces in 2005.
Source: Glasgow Tourism Accommodation Review 2004 / 2005

Volume and value of tourism in Scotland 2003

	Trips (millions)	%	Nights (millions)	%	Expenditure (millions)	%
UK residents	16.5	100	62	100	3,596	100
Overseas residents	1.6	100	14.9	100	837	100

UK and overseas tourism by area tourist boards in Scotland

	UK tourism			Overseas tourism		
Region	Trips	Nights	Spend	Trips	Nights	Spend
Aberdeen and Grampian	9	9	9	7	5	6
Angus and City Dundee	3	3	3	3	3	3
Argyll, The Isles*	13	13	11	13	7	7
Ayrshire and Arran	6	7	5	5	4	4
Dumfries and Galloway	6	5	4	2	1	1
Edinburgh and Lothians	21	15	22	51	34	33
Greater Glasgow and Clyde Valley	18	13	17	31	23	22
Highlands of Scotland	14	16	14	22	13	13
Kingdom of Fife	4	4	3	6	6	6
Perthshire	5	5	5	6	4	5
Scottish Borders	3	2	2	2	1	1
Edinburgh	18	13	20	49	21	30
Glasgow	16	11	15	27	11	18

* Includes Loch Lomond, Sterling and the Trossachs

Northern Ireland

It is important to note that the tourism figures relate to the following. All are state visitors to Northern Ireland, visiting for any reason (holiday, business, visiting friends and relatives) and staying for at least one night. Added to this are Northern Ireland residents on holiday at home. Day trips are not included.

Volume and tourist spending in Northern Ireland 2005

	Trips/Visits millions	Nights millions	Spending £ millions
Tourists	1.967	9.57	354

Regional tourism estimates 2004

	Trips 000s	%	Nights 000s	%	Spend £ millions
Belfast	845.8	27.9	2917.3	25.0	118.3
Derry	166.1	5.5	765.2	6.6	27.1
Fermanagh Lakelands	158.6	5.2	552.8	4.7	25.9
Kingdoms of Down	480.2	19.9	1972.2	16.9	69.7
Causeway Coast and Glens	779.1	25.7	2928.2	25.1	99.0
Sperrins Area	146.3	4.8	722.0	6.2	25.4
Other	450.6	14.9	1818.9	15.6	63.3
Total	3026.7	100	11676.6	100	428.7

Sources: Northern Ireland Passenger Survey – Northern Ireland Tourist Board

The Republic of Ireland

As an indication, the 2004 overseas tourists visits to Ireland increased by 3.3% to 6.4%, exceeding the volume of tourist arriving in Ireland during 2000 the previous record year.

Volume and tourist spending in the Republic of Ireland 2004

	Trips/Visits millions	Spending € millions
Domestic	7001	5105.2
Total overseas	6384	3234.9

Regional tourism estimates

Numbers (000) revenue € millions	Overseas tourists	Northern Ireland	Domestic	Total
Dublin	3,680	192	976	4,848
	1,163	64.6	144	1,371
Midlands/East	777	30	873	1,680
	248	7.1	90.3	345.8
South-East	974	11	1,113	2.098
	267	2.6	152	420
South-West	1,578	51	1,428	3.057
	652	22.6	248.0	922
Shannon	1,075	54	791	1,920
	281	14.1	111	406
West	1,250	43	1,251	2544
	460	15.7	210	686
North-West	487	234	569	1,290
	162	56.4	83	302
Total	3,235	183.1	1,037	4,455

Source: CSO/Fáilte Ireland/NITB

Channel Islands

Volume and tourist spending in the Channel Islands 2005

	Visitors millions	Nights millions	Spending £ millions
UK and overseas residents	16	125	9

The Isle of Man

Volume and tourist spending in the Isle of Man 2005

	Visitors millions	Nights millions	Spending £ millions
UK and overseas residents	12	124	5

SUMMARY

In summary, global trends indicate that people travelling in the future will take more short-break holidays than ever before. This is due to several different factors, among them the trickle-down effect of changes in the workplace and by choice. Visitors will be better educated and more affluent, with high expectations of customer service and value for money.

DOMESTIC MARKET

During 2005, the short-break domestic market had an estimated value of £7.5bn. Inbound visits for business and to visit friends and relatives are forecast to grow more strongly than holiday visits. For more information see VisitBritain web site.

> **TIP**
>
> Be sure you read up on the country of origin when your guests are from overseas.

The number of domestic trips undertaken by the general public is projected to expand for the future. Again, due to changes in the workplace, people will take more short breaks than ever before.

Stress in the workplace is already starting to produce a knock-on effect in personal relationships and subsequently, people will take more time out with their loved ones if only to resolve any rifts that might be emerging.

Holiday patterns are starting to change. Where in the past, holidaymakers predominately took elongated weekends they are now finding that someone in their family may be employed on a part time basis during the weekend, so they will have to take some of their break during the week. For the future, many accommodation businesses will start to notice more evenness throughout the week as people take breaks to fit in with a deregulated workplace.

The next three tables are typical of what you find when clicking onto the various web sites belonging to the tourism authorities. They show the holiday patterns, seasonality and accommodation choice.

Holiday tourism

	Trips/visits (millions)	%	Nights (millions)	%	Spending (£millions)	%
Short (1–2 nights)	3.6	57	7.6	30	465.8	41
Long (4+ nights)	2.6	43	17.8	70	664.3	59

Seasonality

	UK residents % of trips	Overseas residents % of visits
Jan, Feb, Mar	15	14
Apr, May, Jun	29	32
Jul, Aug, Sept	34	39
Oct, Nov, Dec	20	16

Accommodation type 2004

United Kingdom	Visits (000)	Nights (000)	Spend (£m)	Sample size
Hotel/Guest houses	11.451	45,291	5,826	18,716
Bed & Breakfast	1,177	8,576	481	1,570
Republic of Ireland	Visits (000)	Nights (000)	Spend (£m)	Sample size
Hotel/Guest houses	822	2,023	297	685
Bed & Breakfast	106	447	35	80

© Crown Copyright: Office for National Statistics 'International Passenger Survey'

SHORT-BREAK HOLIDAYS

The short-break market has become increasingly significant in recent years with current tourism trends throughout the world moving in favour of one- to three-night breaks rather than fortnightly holidays. Here is what Scottish Tourism has to say:

> Recent research by nVision shows that 50% of UK adults took a UK short-break holiday in 2005 up from 44% in 2003. Short breaks abroad are also on the increase with 31% taking one in 2005, up from 26% in 2003.

The traditional two-week summer holiday is becoming less important for many people. There are thought to be a number of social trends affecting the marketplace, including, for example:

◆ The 'time-squeeze' phenomenon – many people feel they have shorter windows of time in which to take holidays.

◆ Household size is falling – people have more to spend and are less constrained by school holidays.

◆ An ageing population – with more time to take more breaks.

These social trends have already changed the nature of tourism.

The tourism statistics above are a guide only but they will assist you in matching the tourist size by volume and expenditure against the region where you wish to establish a Bed & Breakfast.

All tourist authorities have their own web sites where you can gather meaningful information to help you do your homework.

3

Who Is Your Customer?

This chapter is all about focusing on whom you believe will be your customer. Why do you need to work this out now? Before you decide where you buy, what you are going to buy, or what renovations you will need to convert your existing property, you must know if the market – or customer base – can support your endeavour.

GETTING YOUR FACTS STRAIGHT

How do you go about finding the size of your potential market? If you have not been involved in tourism before, then you will have a limited idea about why people come into your area, or for that matter, what your geographical location has to offer.

The starting point is to source where reliable information can be gathered on key issues such as location, costs, staff requirements, time constraints and a whole host of operating details. At this stage, potential Bed & Breakfast operators need answers, that is, facts and details upon which they can build a comprehensive picture of their proposed operation, the possible market, the methods of operation, etc. They need to undertake research to give them a realistic understanding of their prospective business.

Your Bed & Breakfast will not appeal to everybody. You should be identifying the type of guests you want to attract, that is, your preferred **target market**.

What type of guests would you like to attract to your B&B? The choice is yours – you should at this early stage make this decision. Would you prefer to be servicing the top end of the market or the general holidaymaker? Would you feel more comfortable with corporate clients or with family groups or groups of friends? Your choice of target market will be a vital factor in influencing your decision on where to locate and what type of guest your Bed & Breakfast will attract. Here are ten categories of target guests to help you to identify your prime market group:

- Affluent guests

- Couples

- Singles

- Families

- Corporate

- Guests with a disability

- Budget market

- Groups

- Gays/lesbian

- Guest with pets

Having identified your preferred market groups (this can also indicate age and income), you can now decide whether you are looking at a purely commercial venture, or if you are considering a life-style adjustment still using your existing dwelling. You have two clear options:

1. A **commercial venture** – is a stand-alone business where the income is your prime source of revenue.

2. A **life-style adjustment** – is when you decide to get into Bed & Breakfast as a means of generating a top-up or secondary income and as a *sea-change or tree-change* option. This may well become a source of prime income in the future.

Once your decision has been made as to what type of Bed & Breakfast business you want to run, we suggest a visit to your local tourist information centre to get the most recent facts and figures on how many visitors your preferred area attracts per year. In doing so, you will find out how old they are, what they do, how long they stay, what and why they are visiting. The centre should also be able to advise you on how many other accommodation suppliers are in your area, their average occupancy rate, and any other information regarding the visitors to your area.

Contact your regional tourism boards. They can give you up-to-date information on the type of holidays and accommodation people are choosing in your area. You should be able to ascertain the trends that are occurring. If you notice discrepancies when comparing the data collected, you might be able to bridge or fill any gaps. You can obtain the latest tourism trends, as it applies to your area, by using the contact addresses listed in Useful Addresses (at the back of the book).

FAST FACTS

The following are some facts that will help to put the information you are seeking into some context. It could also be some assistance with various sections of your **feasibility study** or **business plan**.

Research indicates that over the next five years, the domestic market will continue to take more short-break holidays, usually two nights and three days, with more frequency than ever before. Many people surveyed said they would be undertaking this break with their partner, but without children. Fifty per cent said this break would be in their own country.

Many times more women are travelling for both leisure and business as their roles in the workplace become more significant.

Progressively, more people will use the Internet to book holidays and these will often be last minute bookings after destinations and prices have been compared. They will be seeking new experiences and a better understanding of the culture in the areas visited. More visitors are choosing their destinations based on their specific interests, for example, researching family history.

Tourism is predicted to grow substantially in the coming years, with the annual world-spending on all leisure and business travel expected to double to £3 trillion over the next eight years.

The tourism industry in the UK is currently worth around £76 billion, which is more than 4% of the UK's gross domestic product.

There are a few other things you should be aware of. As we know, the world is constantly changing. Rapid and geographically unbalanced economic growth have been predicted to come to an end in the middle of this century. Over this period, the world is predicted to move from the present situation of income inequality, with low average wages, to reasonable income equality, with much higher average income.

Between now and 2050 the world's income is forecast to increase ten-fold. The largest economies will be in Asia. However, among the ten biggest economies, per capita income is expected to remain the highest in the USA.

The key demographic development is the death rate. If, as some people maintain, average life expectancy will move to about 100 years, the world's population may stabilise at approximately ten billion. However, if medical causes of death are lessened by medical progress, then world population may pass ten billion, and keep rising for some time, at about one billion per decade. People are living longer. And there are far more of them. This means two things for you. Retired people need something to supplement their income in their golden years – which in effect could be 30–40 years.

And they will want somewhere to go on a short-break holiday within a two- to three-hour driving distance from their home, Bed & Breakfasts being a favoured accommodation choice.

It is projected that by the year 2010, more than 34% of the UK and Irish workforce could be employed on a part time basis. This means that those of us, who for the future, want to earn the same income that we currently enjoy, will need to have two or three part-time jobs. These won't necessarily be in the same industry. People will have to up-skill in order to get these jobs. To be one of the 66% still employed full time you will need to be highly skilled and trained and be willing to further your education at every opportunity.

Rather than face this ultra-competitive job market, many older (and some younger) people are becoming consultants or contractors. Instead, however, of falling into the 1980's trap of renting an expensive office in a good suburb, they are working out of their high-tech office at home. B&Bs are a great way to help supplement the peaks and troughs of a consultancy business, if your property is in a suitable location.

We have found that 75% of people who are exploring the idea of entering the Bed & Breakfast market are corporate workers doing so as a financial contingency plan for their future. The other 25% do so for emotional reasons. Bed & Breakfasts are a soft financial risk. You may own your own home. If you don't get a lot of bookings you still own your home – you haven't lost your financial shirt.

What about retailing as a way to earn an income after 40? Recent studies found that 50% of all boutique retailers barely cover their rent and their employees' wages.

The hours spent out of their home in their shop increases every year, as consumers want to shop when they are not working. Remember, we are all working longer and, increasingly, deregulated hours. This brings us to another point in the B&B's favour.

Traditionally people worked 9 to 5, Monday to Friday. If you owned a Bed & Breakfast that focused on the domestic market, then your business was restricted, primarily, to weekends. With the increase of flexible working hours and the decrease of the mid-year, two- to three-week holiday, more people are choosing several short holiday breaks throughout the year, often midweek, or as an adjunct to their weekend.

It is estimated that 65% of people had not taken all their accrued holidays in the past year. Of these 36% of people had not taken any leave in the past year, with more than half not having had a holiday for more than two years. Job security concerns are being touted as the likely reason for this, the trend being that people are much more comfortable having a short-break holiday than leaving their office for extended periods. Employers and governments are being pressured into encouraging their employees to take leave.

> **TIP**
>
> Keep yourself up to date with the short-break holiday trends. This market segment is gathering pace.

CAPTURING YOUR TARGET MARKET

So how can you capture this market? Make no mistake about it – to be a success at Bed & Breakfast you need to capture it.

Bed & Breakfasts in cities are becoming a more and more attractive option. Being close to a business district is becoming a desirable location. There needs to be a reason to go to your area, something to do as well as rest.

Are you near a national park and walking tracks or close to a tourist area, the Lake District, Snowdonia, Loch Ness, the Southern Irish Coast, or the Giant's Causeway? Are you in a popular country town: St. Ives, Keswick, Inverness, Abergavenny, Banbridge or Waterford? Are you in a high-density commercial area? These are the factors you need to consider before you start.

If you want to attract a particular type of person, for example, executives visiting your city for conferences, make sure that they will feel at home with you and your partner or family. Ideally, your target market should be people like you, or who like the things you like. In the long run your business will be a greater success.

You also need to ensure that your proposed customer comes into your area in reasonable numbers. Have you checked that they are coming to your area now?

If you want to attract **business** or **corporate clients** you will need to look at your local community and its market potential. Are companies attracted to your area for conferences? Is your local council doing a lot to attract businesses to relocate to your area? You need to ensure your council and tourist office understands the service you can provide, for example, being able to show these visitors the 'real' experience of your community.

Have you thought about academics? Does your town have a **university** or a **tertiary college**? Introduce yourself to the person responsible for booking the accommodation for these visitors, send them your promotional literature and *invite them to come and stay for a night*. If they enjoy their stay they are more likely to book with you.

If, like many B&Bs, you see your market to be **overseas guests**, you need to investigate why tourists are attracted to your area. Is it the local markets? Historic areas? The best beach on the coast of Cornwall, or the pubs? While determining this, by visiting your tourist centre for their research on visitor numbers, you also need to find out the age of the people visiting your area. This information will help you to determine the facilities you need to provide to attract this market. It also helps you to spend your promotional budget wisely.

NICHE MARKETS

This brings us to niche markets. Within the tourist sector you may want to specialise in a particular type of tourist, usually a person who is attracted specifically to your area, or **shares your interest or passion**. Some examples would be fishermen, hikers, birdwatchers and history buffs.

To target a particular niche you may need to consider the following:

- *You have particular knowledge of that market yourself.* If your area is known for its fauna and flora and you intend to exploit this market, you will need to know about this yourself. It would help if you had contact with a naturalist or a local ranger, who could give guided walks or hold weekend workshops for visitors.

- *You may need to supply special facilities.* If your passion is cooking and you are going to run a creative cooking school, you may need to change the layout of your kitchen in order to support this.

- *You might look at special décor.* If your niche is going to be trout fisherman you may want to consider attractive photos in your hallway of local fishing spots, or display a mounted trophy. A word of caution here. Don't go overboard, as you don't want to put other guests off. A few details here and there will provide a conversation point.

Promotion

You need to launch your entry into the market with advertising and editorial in appropriate journals. Offer influential people and decision makers within your niche community a weekend away at your Bed & Breakfast. It is positive word of mouth that will assist in promoting your speciality.

There are major groups that people are targeting with great success. We will discuss them now in detail.

THE CORPORATE MARKET

Some B&B operators capture the **corporate market** midweek and the leisure market during the weekends. If you have travelled extensively on business then you would agree that the part we all detested was dining by ourselves! Bed & Breakfasts can supply the corporate traveller with a degree of normality during their trip.

Some larger Bed & Breakfasts and guest houses are targeting corporate business to stage strategy meetings at their establishment. To do this successfully you need the right facilities, for example: meeting room, computers for PowerPoint demonstrations, slide machines, white boards, markers, photocopiers, faxes, full catering facilities, etc. For larger establishments this can be quite lucrative. Your guests will probably

> **TIP**
> Real estate agents and community organisations such as Rotary and Lions Clubs are a good source to access the corporate market.

want to check their email so an additional phone line would be useful.

SINGLE TRAVELLERS

There are, in many countries, many single people who only talk to people at work; they go home by themselves, to themselves. They need a holiday too, even if it is just to meet and talk to others. Single travellers often want to know the real heart of a city or town and meeting the locals is part of that. What better way to meet the locals than stay in their home? You need to be centrally located and close to transport. You will not win any points if your guest needs to travel through poorly lit, suburban streets to reach the local bus stop or train station.

Please do single travellers a favour and don't banish them to your smallest, dingiest room. Remember that the single traveller is paying more per head than your average couple, and they are eating less, using less electricity and hot water. Treat them well and they will return the favour, recommending you to other single travellers.

WOMEN TRAVELLERS

The **single female traveller** is an ever-growing market – both as part of work and as part of adventure. Some women, however, feel uncomfortable sitting by themselves having dinner. If they go to a restaurant alone they are in danger of attracting unwanted attention from the opposite sex, or they feel trapped in their room if they order room service. Bed & Breakfasts are a great antidote to this, particularly those that offer the option of an evening meal.

For the single woman the Bed & Breakfast offers conversation without pressure as well as a homely touch. Some Bed & Breakfasts are targeting the corporate end of this market quite successfully, appealing to the safety angle and the gregarious nature of women. Remember if you are going to try for this market it can be difficult to access from the suburbs. An inner city location, close to good restaurants, attractions and transport, would be a viable option.

ALTERNATIVE LIFESTYLE

The so-called 'pink pound' is often talked about as a lucrative market and, of course, some Bed & Breakfasts are run by gay couples. Your customers are often well paid with a high disposable income.

Word of mouth works very strongly here. You could alert potential visitors by advertising in the gay press. The Internet is also another powerful tool for this market. Your customers are usually tech-savvy and will use their computers to book their short breaks. This market is not for everyone, but if you're comfortable with it, and it must be said that **if you are going to run a Bed & Breakfast you will need to be open minded**, you will have a loyal customer base here.

PEOPLE WITH A DISABILITY

This group, like any other, both likes to travel for pleasure and needs to travel with work. Remember that only a small percentage of people who come under this heading use a wheelchair. They do, however, often have **special needs**. If you are purpose-building a Bed & Breakfast you might like to consider this group. You will have some statutory requirements to adhere to, so we suggest strongly that you obtain a copy of the appropriate Act from the Stationery Office or download it free of charge at: www.disability.gov.uk

Again this is a very loyal group, with great word of mouth potential. If you can cater to their special needs they will frequent your B&B. You will find that many of the modifications you will make for the disabled are also good for the elderly.

DIETARY REQUIREMENTS

Some Bed & Breakfasts have had success with guests with particular dietary requirements, for example, vegan, gluten-free, vegetarian and kosher. We would suggest you only try to cater for these groups if you share their predilections, as they want meals that are tasty. Usually, only someone who understands their needs has the ability to cater for such groups.

FAMILY MARKET

There is a growing need for some Bed & Breakfasts to cater specifically for the family market with the development of well designed suites that can serve the multi-purpose of family and group accommodation, and can also revert to separate accommodation. The biggest opportunities are for those who are located in an area where there is a lot for children to do: swim, fish, ride horses, walk, visit historic sites and be close to a major attraction, etc.

Self-contained cottages, where the host provides a breakfast, often in the form of a basket meal, is becoming a very popular choice for families. At the moment most Bed & Breakfasts are giving this market to caravan parks, which are refurbishing and building cabins at a rapid rate. B&B operators who cater for this market should do well, given that it is generally accepted as being affordable.

You will need to contact your relevant local authority before considering self-catering accommodation.

Another popular place to cater for families is a Bed & Breakfast on a farm. If you go down this road you need to create almost a storybook farm on your property, with sheep, cats, dogs, pigs and chickens children can feed, ponies they can ride, and a cow or a goat the children can hand milk. All this with appropriate adult supervision, of course. For the city child this would represent the adventure of a lifetime. Be sure to talk to your insurance provider if you plan to offer activities such as these.

Some authorities will require specific zoning before you will be allowed to go ahead. We suggest that you obtain a copy of your relevant local government and housing requirements to see whether your property is suitably classified.

DO'S AND DON'TS

In this age of litigation we wanted to explore how the Bed & Breakfast operator is affected by advertising 'No smoking', 'No children', and 'No pets'. Various government departments were contacted to try to ascertain how the Bed & Breakfast operator was placed in relation to these exclusions and to anti-discrimination laws. We found that government departments tend to be reactive, rather than proactive. In other words, they will wait until a member of the public makes a complaint about any restriction before making a judgement.

There are many strategies you can adopt in order to handle difficult situations should they arise.

NO PETS

There are hygiene and health, not to mention safety reasons, why you should not allow pets in your B&B unless you have suitable accommodation for them. If you have your own pets you will need to advertise this to potential guests. There may be valid reasons why guests prefer to stay where there are no pets. For example, they may be allergic to them. Have handy the name of a local kennel that houses cats and dogs so that you can recommend them to potential guests.

Some B&Bs, however, are successfully targeting this market and acting as hosts for animals. You would need to clearly map out your intentions to your local authority to ensure that you have all areas covered before you advertise the fact. You should also advise your insurers that you are catering for animals as it may have an effect on your annual premium.

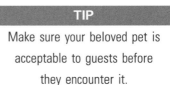

TIP

Make sure your beloved pet is acceptable to guests before they encounter it.

NO SMOKING

We believe that this is a valid 'don't'. Smoke gets into fabrics and furnishings and is impossible to remove completely before new guests arrive. However, we would suggest that you provide a sheltered area outside where your guests can smoke. Provide an ashtray (which you clean at least twice daily) and a small rubbish bin. This will stop butts littering your garden. When advising potential guests of your property inform them of your policy, but let them know about the outside area.

The Health and Safety at Work Act 1974 and regulations require employers to ensure, as far as is reasonably practicable, the health, safety and welfare of all their staff when at work. This could include taking steps to protect workers from illness caused by passive smoking. Where rest facilities are provided for staff, a smoke-free area must be available for non-smokers.

NO CHILDREN

This is the tricky one. The Anti-Discrimination Act (see below) prohibits discrimination on account of age. Blankly saying, 'No children allowed' or 'Children not welcome' will be seen as you discriminating against an age group. This can be a dilemma however, as you will find that some guests who want to experience selected types of accommodation do so to have a break together. You may choose only to cater for families with children at certain times, for example school holidays.

If you don't wish children to stay it is better to say: 'We don't have the facilities to cater for children'. If you do want to welcome children this could be developed as an interesting and lucrative niche market. But remember children will behave like children and you need to be prepared for what that may mean.

We also suggest that you obtain a free copy of the 'Children Act' titled, *A guide to help you with day registration* or download at www.doh.gov.uk/busguid/childact.htm

ANTI-DISCRIMINATION AND THE BED & BREAKFAST HOST

Over the last few years there has been an increase in discussion of the rights of smokers, children, and the disabled. In a society that is becoming more litigious, B&B operators need to know their position in light of new developments in anti-discrimination. Do Bed & Breakfast operators have special rights in light of the fact that they live on the premises and their business is also their home? In researching this we came up with the following items of interest:

Question: Is there a law that would prohibit B&B operators from having a 'no children as guests', policy? For example, they may not have adequate facilities to cater for young children.

Answer: All government areas have what they call 'Parental Status and an Aging Policy' which states quite clearly that no one in business can discriminate on age. If your B&B preference were not to have minors as guests, then to say that you don't have facilities for children would not be enough to stop a prospective guest from lodging a discrimination complaint against you. You can, however, apply for an exemption to this ruling. Your argument would need to be very well thought through and soundly based to have any chance of succeeding. One could consider saying, 'Our property is not suitable for children as there are no facilities to keep them entertained'. In this way you have warned the reader in your advertisement that the children might not have enough to keep them occupied. Most parents on reading comments like that would select another property.

Question: Does the law require a B&B operator to provide wheelchair access?

Answer: Wheelchair access is not mandatory as some dwellings are not suitable for this type of access by their very nature, but again, there are no grounds to discriminate against someone who uses a wheelchair and wishes to stay at your B&B. It is implicit in this situation that means of accessing the facilities are within the reach of your guest.

Question: Can a B&B operator enforce a 'no smoking' policy?

Answer: You can specify no smoking on your property by placing 'Thank you for not smoking.' signs in appropriate areas. There does not appear to be a law that states you *can't* specify no smoking although this, as with many areas of the Anti-discrimination Act, needs to be tested in the courts.

Question: Is it reasonable for a B&B operator to take the following view: 'Because my B&B is the place where I live, I can set policy and make rules that would not be possible if the property was a large hotel or guest house'?

Answer: Not really, if it means that discrimination factors are ignored and the law is broken. Common sense should prevail when dealing with these issues because litigation is both lengthy and costly. By couching your words more carefully, when advertising features pertaining to your B&B, readers will be able to decide whether your Bed & Breakfast property is suitable for their situation. In considering this point, remember that people do not appreciate being misled. It is important that you keep abreast of anti-discrimination policy and subscribe to publications that can enlighten you on the issues that concern you and your Bed & Breakfast.

TIP

As you collect information on your area, brochures, books and the like, keep them for later use. Guests will appreciate reading books on the history of your area, great walks, local attractions, etc.

4

Preparing Your Property

T he first decision you need to make when entering the short
break holiday market is whether you are going to be a
'traditional' Bed & Breakfast with a few rooms and a cosy
atmosphere. Or will you be a guest house or a small hotel, where
there is more separation between you and your guests? The
difference is governed by statutory requirements in some places and
only you can make the decision as to how you wish to operate.

The main reason people choose the traditional Bed &
Breakfast option is because the house they currently own has
suffient space to accommodate both themselves and potential
guests. There are benefits: your guests have easy access to you, it
is easier to keep an eye on your property, it is not as far to go to
work. The negatives are that having a family life can be
constrained by your guests, that you need to be conscious that
guests can access your personal space, and it is hard to ever
escape from work.

What is the best option? The main thing you need to consider is
privacy. No matter which route you choose – or due to property
or financial constraints, have chosen for you – you need to ensure

you and your family have some personal space where guests are unable to intrude. This is a statutory requirement throughout Ireland.

Your family area would include a bathroom, bedrooms and preferably a separate lounge or family room. Without this space the strain on your personal relationships may be too much to bear. It is also good for your guests, as they are less likely to feel they are intruding on another's life. This space is particularly important if you have children or grandchildren living with you.

LOCATION

Position, position! For many reasons this could be the single most important part of establishing a successful Bed & Breakfast.

The position of your Bed & Breakfast in relation to your market really could make the difference as to whether your enterprise will succeed or fail. An important factor to remember is that guests often like to be within walking distance of food and drink.

To determine whether your property is in the right position, remember to consider both people on touring holidays as well as those who are having a short-break holiday, the latter often within a short driving time from their home. International guests tend to look for properties that are close to public transport facilities.

To be a roaring success, with good occupancy, you need to appeal to both markets. Ask yourself the following questions about your property or the one you are thinking of purchasing:

* Is my property near a main road or in a country town with easy access?

* Is my property close to a tourist area? Factor into your profit and loss projections the seasonality of the area and the likelihood your bookings may fluctuate.

* Is my property within a large metropolitan city? Be sure your property is aimed at an appropriate market if it is in a suburban area and that it is well signposted, as your guests will not want to spend all their time finding you. It is best to be close to public transport, especially for those guests who are touring, and to popular attractions. If you are targeting the corporate market your guests will need good access to, and to be within easy travelling distance of the business district.

LOCAL GOVERNMENT AND YOUR BED & BREAKFAST

Before you march headlong into deciding where you are going to set up your Bed & Breakfast, or whether you are going to convert your current home, you need to establish a relationship with your local authority.

Firstly, there is a raft of planning permission and building regulation that can apply to those offering serviced or self-catering accommodation. As an example, if you are considering structural changes to an existing dwelling or adding an extension, it is vital that you contact your local authority for their advice and/or permission.

Policies on granting planning permission do vary, for example, on car parking facilities and guest room numbers. Even if you feel that your home has the facilities set down by local authorities, a 'change of use' planning permission may still be required.

Another suggestion is to get a copy of the relevant authority's planning approval guide.

For those of you who are planning something a little more ambitious you might want to hire a consultant to act on your behalf. At their worst, relevant authorities can require mountains of documentation and it can save a lot of heartache if you hire a professional.

If you want to make a complaint against the handling of your application, you should firstly contact the authority itself. If you are still dissatisfied, lodge a complaint with a higher authority. When there is conflict it is best to be guided by your own legal advice or that of a private planning consultant.

TO CONVERT, BUY OR BUILD?

You need to establish whether you are going to convert the home you already live in, buy a new place, or custom-build a property if you can find suitable land.

Each option has its merits – what you choose will depend on your personal circumstance. If you only want your Bed & Breakfast to give you pocket money, a supplement to an already healthy financial position, we would suggest you convert the property you already have. If you want your B&B to provide you with a little more financially, and if your house is not in a major city or a tourist area you may need to consider either buying an existing property or custom-building one.

> **TIP**
>
> Consider self-contained cottages if you have young children as you will maintain greater privacy and reduce the chance of burnout.

AN EXERCISE IN FINANCIAL VIABILITY

To test the viability of getting your house ready for a Bed & Breakfast the following can be used as a benchmark. Using your note-book go into all the areas of your property that guests will encounter, taking notes about what needs doing in each of these spaces. Be sure to look at these areas through the **eyes of a paying guest** or ask someone else to do it for you. If you do this exercise through the eyes of the resident property owner you will be in danger of deluding yourself. You are going into Bed & Breakfast to succeed. Therefore you need to view the property as a potential guest and so charge as much as possible, without being excessive. In this way the maximum occupancy that you can comfortably handle can be realised. You will not achieve these goals if your product is not right.

You need to look at the following in every room:

Ceiling
- Is the ceiling flaking?
- Are there any damp patches?
- Does it need repainting?

Walls
- Is the paintwork in good condition and painted a colour that adds to the ambiance of a guest bedroom and the look of your B&B?
- Are there cracks or any structural problems?
- Will you have to strip wallpaper or replace it?

Flooring
- Is your carpet or flooring in good condition or does it need shampooing or polishing?

◆ If the floor is polished timber then do you need to revarnish or stain?

General

◆ How soundproof is your house? This is particularly important in bedrooms, as nothing is more off-putting, or uncomfortable, than being aware of other people's more intimate moments.
◆ Is there adequate ventilation?
◆ Is there adequate lighting?
◆ Are there any structural problems?
◆ Is there enough space to give every guest bedroom an en suite or bathroom? If your room rate is going to be high your guests' expectation would be their very own fully equipped guest bathroom, possibly even with a spa bath.
◆ Is there enough storage area or wardrobe space in each guest bedroom?
◆ Is there appropriate fire safety installed? In most instancies a regular, legal inspection is required.
◆ Is there adequate hot water?

Later in this chapter we discuss all the extras you will need to consider when converting your house into a Bed & Breakfast.

Once you have decided what work you need to do, ascertain what work you can do yourself and where you will need a professional. Obviously, the more you can do yourself the better off you will be financially. The things you need professionals for should be listed. You then need to get at least three quotes for everything. It is worth the time and the effort.

After you have done all this, you need to compare the cost with a projection of what you think you can earn. How much is too much money? As a general rule, you should only spend what you think you can get back when selling your property as a house, not as a Bed & Breakfast.

TIPS FOR BUYING AN ESTABLISHED B&B

You have done the research and realised that your home just won't adequately convert to a Bed & Breakfast. Plus you have decided that you want to make this your sole livelihood. You have a bit of money in the bank and you believe the best thing to do is buy an established Bed & Breakfast. That way you should have a good income from day one.

When looking to purchase an established Bed & Breakfast you need to consider the following:

- Why is the business for sale?
- Is the area the Bed & Breakfast is in overpopulated with accommodation providers and therefore bookings are low?
- Are the owners experiencing B&B burnout? (It happens!)
- Do they have children who have reached teenage years and the lifestyle is just too difficult to juggle?
- Is there a motorway or other development to be built which will affect the area?

The first and last reasons are what you need to consider. The middle ones could mean you might have a viable property.

- How old is the business and how many of the years have been profitable? Have they been making a profit for the last couple of years?

- How much business is currently booked for the next 6 months? Ask to see the reservation diary. Ask to see the visitors' book. Guests don't lie. If the business is well loved you should see it from the book. It also helps you understand what the guests love about the place. Is the success tied up in the current owners? The cooking? The nearby historical sights? The architecture of the house?

- What percentage of the Bed & Breakfast's business is made up of return customers? How much, therefore, are you paying for 'goodwill', that is, the intangible contribution of the current owners? Is it valid?

- Do the books look accurate? Do the assets outweigh the liabilities? Get the opinion of your solicitor, bank manager, accountant or financial adviser.

- Have all renovations been undertaken with council approval? Is the property zoned for Bed & Breakfast operation?

- As with the purchase of any property location is an important thing to consider. You cannot be in an area where the reasons to stay are too limited for the business to be viable. Does the B&B have the right qualities?

- Is the current operator irretrievably connected to the success of the Bed & Breakfast? Are they award-winning chefs who bring foodies to the establishment? Will your relative lack of culinary expertise be the downfall of the Bed & Breakfast?

CONVERT TO WHAT?

If you are to turn your current house into a B&B you will, undoubtedly, need to make some changes. Guests choose B&Bs for their homely atmosphere, but what they want is the picture book version of home – not the reality.

They don't want the family fights, the untidiness, the laundry, the cooking or cleaning, or the discussions on what to watch on TV. They want the conveniences of a hotel, but with a home-cooked meal, pleasant discussion, and touches such as fresh flowers and home-made biscuits. They want a room filled with good books, a bathroom with complimentary bath salts and oils, and the smell of freshly baked scones and freshly ground coffee. And increasingly they want an en suite or bathroom of their own.

When assessing the changes you will need to make to your property to cater for guests you will need to start from the outside in.

SIGNAGE

The cheapest way you can get your B&B noticed is with a sign. It needs to be in the style of your B&B's architecture, your other promotional material (stationery, etc) and your area. Use a professional signwriter – the sign will create a first impression, and it needs to denote professionalism.

Before contracting a signwriter or graphic designer to work on your behalf you will need to contact your local authority. There are usually regulations on signage placement, height and type and sometimes on colours, particularly if it is illuminated. It's cheaper to find out the restrictions before you are the proud owner of a sign you are unable to display.

It's also a good idea to ensure the name and street number of your establishment is clear to read day or night.

> **TIP**
>
> You never get a second chance to make a first impression. First impressions count.

Nothing puts guests in a worse mood than being unable to find your establishment if your street name or house number is hidden behind a hedge or cannot be read on a dark, wet night.

FIRST IMPRESSIONS COUNT

The first glance your guests have of your B&B will be the **impression** they will take with them. It won't matter what they find on the inside of your establishment, that first look of your unkempt gardens and a dilapidated fence will stay with them throughout their whole stay. That is, if they bother to come in at all.

The truth is, first impressions count. What you can get away with in your own home you cannot get away with as a proprietor of a Bed & Breakfast. The outside appearance of your establishment helps to set the tone of your business. Use the following checklist to help ensure that your first impression is a good one.

- The lawn is mown regularly.
- The path to the front door is free from overgrown bushes and hedges.
- The path is free from cracks and weeds.
- If the house is made of bricks then be sure they are clean.
- Repaint when necessary. When you do repaint, don't paint over a problem. It will recur. Cure the problem first, then paint.
- The fence is in good condition.
- The entrance is free from spider webs.
- Letterboxes, door handles and windows are clean and polished.
- Light bulbs are changed as soon as necessary.
- The outside is well lit at night.

- The garden is regularly attended, with no dead plants.
- Any steps or tiling are swept and cleaned regularly – and checked for slipperiness.
- 🏠 🏠 Signage to car parking and reception is clearly visible.

As for your **garden**, you need it to be as attractive as you can make it. When planning your garden think about the time you can realistically afford to spend maintaining it and design it accordingly.

In the summer months, it is a good idea to have some garden furniture so your guests can enjoy the sunshine and have some outdoor privacy. The advantage of this is it is also a great place for you and your family to also enjoy the sunshine and some privacy.

Think about the addition of a water feature of some sort. Not only are they aesthetically pleasing, but the sound is very soothing – just what you need in a Bed & Breakfast. Not to mention the fact that it is very good feng shui. The Chinese believe that water is the symbol of money. A water feature will help attract more money into your home. (They say!)

> **TIP**
>
> The most important thing about your B&B is to have a spotlessly clean front door step. People always glance down at the front door and spotlessness here gives an impression of care and attention to detail.

YOUR ENTRANCE

Your entrance is the first thing your guests will see on arrival at your establishment. It is your chance to impress them from the word go. You want touches that will exude warmth and friendliness. Go for a huge bunch of fresh flowers, a feature wall in a bright colour or an original piece of artwork. If your hall is narrow it might be a good idea to add a large mirror to help convey a sense of spaciousness.

It is a good idea not to go overboard with furniture in an entrance as it can create an obstacle course when carrying luggage. An umbrella stand and a coat rack or cupboard are ideal additions. You don't want guests traipsing water throughout the house. They will be pleased with your thoughtfulness.

Flooring deserves special consideration in your porch and hallway. You want a surface that is easy to keep clean and is hard wearing. Tiles need to be non-slip, or if you have floorboards you must ensure any polish is not slippery. If you choose carpet you should investigate commercial carpet – it is more durable and easier to keep clean than domestic grade carpets.

Heating or cooling is another consideration. If you are surrounded by snow you want your entry to feel like a warm cocoon. Likewise, if it happens to be hot and humid you want your guests first impression to be one of coolness and freshness.

> **TIP**
>
> Leave a small blackboard ne
> the bell at the front door, wh
> a guest is about to ring they v
> see their name: Helen and
> Warren. It gives the guest a
> warm welcome!

LIVING ROOMS

As we stated in the last chapter, it is important, if at all possible, for both your sanity and your guests' to have some separate space, other than your respective bedrooms. We would suggest that the best option would be a **lounge** room, or similar type of room. For some properties, it might be your old family room, conservatory or former children's playroom. This room will give your guests space and allow them to feel more at home. The fact that you will have a separate lounge room gives you a place to escape that feels all yours, not the property of the general public.

Research indicates that guests don't mind sharing living room areas with each other, providing they can identify where they can sit. For example, if you have a living area available for two guest bedrooms then rearrange your furniture so as you have two settings. You don't want people trapped in their bedroom. Guests generally don't mind if other guests share their space, or even if it is possible to overhear their conversation.

You need **entertainment facilities**, particularly music. An assortment of books is a great idea, covering all genres.

Board games are essential – people love to challenge their friends to a game. **Television** is another thing you will need to consider. Many people go to Bed & Breakfasts to escape from television, but others find it relaxing. My suggestion would be that if you are going to have televisions place them in the guest bedrooms (preferably in a cupboard) where they can make the choice to use them, or have a separate TV room. If, because of space limitations, you have to put a TV in the lounge room, don't arrange all your seating to face it and, preferably, hide it in a cupboard.

Be sure to contact the TV Licensing Authority, as extra TVs may not be covered by your home licence.

One of our concerns is that of 'amenity creep'. Some B&Bs are emulating the atmosphere found in hotels from the lower end of the market. Don't do this, because people who choose to stay in Bed & Breakfasts do so for the homely comforts and to avoid the impersonal atmosphere of a hotel. For example, avoid a TV in a guest bedroom that swivels out from the wall.

People love to sit around an **open fire**, so if you have one, be sure to light it, particularly on dull or cold days. This would be a memorable feature of your lounge room and will be a source of good publicity for you. If you have it, flaunt it.

Likewise, if you have a view of the ocean or mountains, exploit it. These things are what guests go away for – the romantic ideal of home.

DINING ROOMS

As the name suggests, a vitally important part of a B&B is one meal – breakfast. This meal needs to be taken in a place that characterises the ambience of your establishment. As much care should be taken with the dining room as with the bedrooms.

In the United Kingdom and Ireland, B&Bs have taken many different approaches to dining. Many places follow the European tradition of one large table around which all guests sit. This works very well for dinner, if you are planning to offer this as an option. People will occasionally bring their own wine and, over a few glasses, feel happy talking with strangers.

One large, communal table, however, can present some problems at breakfast. Some people are a little shy in the mornings and tend to keep to themselves. A number of establishments have found that they needed to introduce a breakfast area made up of a few tables of two and/or four settings, or a large and a small table.

It is a statutory requirement in some areas to have a separate breakfast table for each guest bedroom.

As for style, you need to create a room that both looks good and is practical. Remember you will be serving breakfast, so you want to be able to access all the seats. The table or tables can become a feature in the dining room, with an interesting centrepiece. Chairs should be comfortable. People on holidays won't want to rush meals so you want them to feel comfortable sitting for as long as they desire.

When buying furniture be aware of the upkeep. If your table is wood it will require work because you will need to protect it from moisture and heat.

When replacing furniture, you should consider new furnishings that meet higher fire resistance standards. Ask your local fire authority if in doubt.

You can get some great buys at places such as second-hand shops. You also have the option of buying from a manufacturer or supplier of commercial catering furniture. For chairs, particularly, this may provide the best option for a larger establishment, as they will be comfortable, practical and hardwearing.

Ensure your dining room has a **sideboard** or bench of some kind. It makes it much easier when clearing tables and serving meals. It also has the added advantage of holding your dinner sets and cutlery. The only word of caution would be not to clutter the top with too many decorative items – keep it simple. If you have too much on it you will find it difficult to use it.

The **crockery** you use can demonstrate to your guests the style of your B&B. Remember it is the small things that your guests will describe to their friends.

Your everyday dinner set, with its scratches, chips and cracks will not do for paying guests. That doesn't mean I'm suggesting you run out and buy Wedgwood or Royal Doulton, although for some of you that might be appropriate.

We would suggest crockery is of commercial quality. Any patterns should be under a thick glaze and able to withstand dishwashers at high temperatures. Tapered edges are more prone to chipping, so if you or your partner are clumsy, we suggest choosing crockery with a rolled edge. Enquire in a retail outlet if there is a piece of china that could be tested for durability. Ask if the retailer has a discarded piece of the china of the type you are interested in purchasing in order to test the glazing, or enquire about guarantees for the durability of the surface. The glazing can be assessed by running a knife across a glazed surface and seeing if it marks. If you see a flaw, keep looking. Do not scrimp on china by buying the cheapest and, whatever you do, don't buy end of line china. Pieces will chip and break and you need a set for which you can easily purchase replacements or additions as required.

Remember you want china that is ovenproof, particularly if you are planning to offer dinner, and any china with a metal embossing, such as a gold rim, may not be suitable to be put in a microwave or a dishwasher.

🏠 🏠 Commercial sets might be a good option for the larger Bed & Breakfasts and guest houses as your crockery may get quite a beating. This doesn't mean you still can't demonstrate personal style. Buy some beautiful serving plates and dishes. Use beautiful cutlery and glasses. Use the best linen napkins you can afford.

Choose a style of china and glassware and linen that reflect the style of your home, and which may be a feature of your region.

Your **glasses** should complement your china. In some cases, where a B&B does not have a liquor licence, guests may be able to bring alcohol, with your permission, whether you provide an evening meal or not. At the very least you will need glasses for red and white wine, sherry, port, champagne, mixed drinks, and water, soft drink or cordial.

Cutlery needs special consideration for your Bed & Breakfast. Again, I would suggest easy care. Stainless steel is much easier to look after than silver, not least because you will be able to put it in the dishwasher. It will still stain and smear, however. To minimise this a good tip is to use boiling hot water and vinegar and wipe it with a linen tea towel once a week after it has been cleaned in a dishwasher.

Ornate designs can look wonderful, but are more difficult to keep clean. Choose cutlery made in one piece as grease and bacteria tend to accumulate between the blade and the handle. Plastic, bone and wooden handles are not always a good idea, as they will not withstand the dishwasher. As you can see, you need to balance style considerations with practical ones. Do you want to be cleaning that beautiful silver cutlery every day? Remember that you do want the table to look special when set, so choose wisely.

THE KITCHEN

While design and size of **kitchen** will vary tremendously in Bed & Breakfasts this is still a main cog in the machine. Your kitchen may be used for cooking only or may have an eat-in function, which, while unsuitable or unlawful for guests, will be great for your family's privacy.

The main thing you need to ensure is **cleanliness**. You are now serving food to the general public and you need to treat this with the seriousness it deserves. The last thing you want is to risk food poisoning. You will need to contact your local authority to see what restrictions will affect you in your kitchen, eg, larger B&Bs must have a separate refrigerator for the guests' food. Increasingly, there is a legal requirement for those preparing food for the general public to obtain a recognised qualification. This will cover all aspects of food handling, storage and preparation. Your local Environmental Health Officer will have all the details.

The larger your establishment, the more likely you will be affected by commercial laws of some kind or another.

Make sure that all of your electrical equipment is safe as you have the responsibility to comply with the regulations set down.

See your local authority about regulations and inspection
requirements.

For health reasons, cutting boards should be labelled. For
example, green for vegetables, red for meat, with matching
colour-coded wiping cloths. Once again, it's a good idea to
obtain a copy of the relevant health and safety legislation to be
sure that your equipment complies with the relevant standards.

When it comes to design you need to remember preparing meals
for a number of guests will require significant workspace such as
a large bench and or table.

As the minimum you will want a dishwasher, a microwave and an
extractor fan. You might also need to consider a bigger fridge,
and a pantry.

The other thing you must consider is safety. Kitchens need to be
safe places in which to work. Kitchens and bathrooms are the
most dangerous places in a home. Flooring needs special
attention, for example, any tiles need to be the non-slip variety.

When it comes to kitchens, local government requirements tend
to vary depending on the number of guest rooms applied for by
the property owner. The best advice is to contact your local
authority before making any drastic changes to your kitchen.
Research shows that there may be changes regarding requirements
for kitchens in the near future.

The average residential B&B would require a double sink and
dishwasher. High quality detergent must be used because the

average dishwasher bought for the home does not heat to 60° Celsius.

For B&Bs that offer an evening meal, they would require all the above, but the dishwasher might need to be semi-industrial.

B&Bs that have an attached dining room with a restaurant will need to comply with standard restaurant regulations.

BATHROOMS AND TOILETS

The days of expecting your guests to share the family **bathroom** are gone. That is not to say you can't be a B&B if you don't have separate bathrooms or en suites for each guest room. However, it means that you may not be able to have a room rate that is viable or an occupancy rate that is acceptable.

Another area to watch is the *new* Star Grading format that requires minium standards example, bathrooms for guests only.

If you do elect to run with the family bathroom proposition then be sure you have sufficient cabinets that hide the family's gear. If it's a grand and elegant B&B you have in mind, and the room rate reflects this, then the guest's expectation will be to access a fully equipped bathroom. This may include a spa bath.

To en suite or not to en suite, that is the question? If you can only afford to do one major thing to convert your family home into a Bed & Breakfast, installing en suites is what you should spend your money on. More bookings are lost for not having en suites than for any other reason, especially with international travellers. Guests will happily pay more for this option.

If you intend to accommodate people with disabilities then the bathroom and toilet facilities will need special consideration. You will need to consider safety rails, a hand-held showerhead and widened doorways. Again, floor tiles need to be non-slip. The relevant authorities will supply you with all the necessary details.

Given that you have heating in your bathroom, you will also need an extractor fan to eradicate all the condensation that occurs. Opening a window is not sufficient to maintain the controlled ventilation required to keep condensation, and in the long term, mould, at bay in bathrooms. If you have sufficient room between your bathroom ceiling and the roof, the most efficient way to cover heating, ventilation and lighting is by installing a three-in-one heater, fan and light. For a little extra expenditure you will have a bathroom that is well lit, warm and well ventilated.

We would suggest that you replace shower curtains with doors, as there is less chance for errant water, and thus accidents. Likewise, as another safety precaution, we would suggest that showers are not over your bath. This is another safety nightmare.

If you must use shower curtains ensure that you wash them regularly. Nothing puts off a guest more than mould. Also ensure they are weighted at the bottom, so they do not wrap around your guests' legs when they are having a shower.

It is important to have efficient, easy to operate showers. Taps with a simple single action are the best. The flow of water from the showerhead also needs to be adequate. It is very hard to rinse long hair with a trickle of water.

You need to ensure you have a copious supply of hot water. This is not an area where one can economise. Guests will always remember the B&B where they had a cold shower, bath or shave, and it will not be looked on favourably when telling their friends of their holiday break.

All the doors should be fitted with locks, and windows should be made of opaque glass or fitted with blinds. Your guests want to feel as if their stay is a retreat and not a peep show. The locks are particularly important if guests are sharing a bathroom.

You also may need to consider adding power points to large bathrooms. Special waterproof points are available and are a legal requirement. At the very least you need sufficient power points for two appliances, a shaver and a hairdryer.

Ideally the bathroom area is self-contained, with the hand basin in the bathroom. This gives a classier atmosphere to the room. A separate toilet with a wash hand basin is also a valuable facility if you have the room.

When it comes to furniture in your bathroom, it should be kept to a minimum. However, you might like to consider a chair or stool. Ensure it won't be affected adversely by the dampness.

With bathrooms and en suites it is the extras that will win you brownie points with your guests. We suggest that you consider providing the following:

◆ Two good quality, generously sized towels per person, which you change daily. You also need to provide a hand towel and two face cloths.

- Mini soaps, preferably from a place like Bodyshop or another aromatherapy retailer. You might even be lucky enough to find a local person who makes natural products. These will need to be changed after each guest. The provision of a soap dispenser is a good alternative.

- Make-up remover pads. This is a great idea, as it will prevent your guests using your towels for this purpose.

- Plenty of thick, luxurious-feeling, toilet paper. OK, so it's a hidden luxury. So many Bed & Breakfasts get this wrong. Don't scrimp and buy the cheap brand. Your guests will notice and will not be impressed. Ensure your spare rolls are in an easy-to-find place.

- Candles, and some matches. These are particularly recommended if you have a spa. Nothing is more relaxing or romantic than candlelight, and isn't romance one of the main reasons your guests have chosen the Bed & Breakfast experience?

- Fresh flowers, preferably from your garden, or a small plant, will brighten up the room and reinforce the impression that you are the nurturing type. Be aware that some guests may be allergic to fresh flowers, so you may want to advise them beforehand or be prepared to remove them.

- A hair dryer: forgetful guests will love you for this.

- A waste bin with a lid: the more bins you provide the less mess you will need to tidy up later.

- Complimentary bath oils, shower caps, shampoos and conditioners. These are a real treat and everyone loves them.

THE BEDROOMS

If you are going after the luxury romantic getaway market you might consider having spa baths for each guest bedroom. At the high end of the market, they are a definite draw card. You can, of course, get a higher room rate for the privilege.

There are now minimum bedroom size and spaciousness requirements that are as follows:

*   single rooms   5.6sq m/60sq ft
*   double rooms   8.4sq m/90sq ft
*   twin rooms   10.2sq m/110sq ft.

Now to the 'bed' part of your B&B, the place where your guests will spend at least one third of their stay with you.

The first points of call are the beds. This is the most important investment in furniture you will make – and you really must consider buying new ones. It is your guests' opinion of the quality of your bed you will most be recommended for.

One of the most common questions we are asked is what should you look for when purchasing a bed. Firstly – buy wholesale. As soon as you register your business you will gain allowances with a wide range of wholesalers, from bed linen and bed manufacturers, to hospitality suppliers. Take advantage of these and shop around.

We also suggest you buy contract quality. These beds have the added advantage of being built for multiple and varied sleepers – so they will last longer in the long run. Most importantly they are reinforced around the sides – the first place your guests will sit when entering their guest room.

If you have a number of guest rooms, purchase queen beds, doubles are too small for most couples, and have at least one room with two single beds that will zip up into a queen- or king-size bed. With more and more friends travelling together, along with mothers and daughters and colleagues, the ability to offer twin beds will give your potential guests another reason to stay with you.

The Star Grading system calls for minimum bed sizes. For example, a single bed must not be smaller than: 190×90cm/6ft 3in $\times$ 4ft. A double bed should be: 190×137cm/6ft 3in $\times$ 4ft 6in.

Beds of 183×75cm/6ft $\times$ 2ft 6in will only be acceptable for children in a family room. Beds of 190×122cm/6ft 3in $\times$ 4ft are acceptable for single occupancy only.

Bunk beds that cannot be used by adults must have a 75cm/2ft 6in clear space between the mattress of the bottom bed and the underside of the top bed (Bunk Bed Regulations 1997).

Note: It's advisable to download the Star Grading program from your preferred tourism authority in order to be sure that you have met all minimum requirements.

As for brands, we recommend Sealy. Why? They understand the needs of the hospitality industry, including B&Bs. The coverings all meet the UK furniture industry's stringent regulations. The single zip up model has the option of an all-over covering. All their commercial beds are Healthshield protected, which protects against the build up of mould, mildew, bacteria and dust mites. The coverings are fire retardant. Sealy also provide a service that will show you how to care for the bed in the longer term. Their contract division, which will deal directly with you, can provide you with substantial savings.

A rack or suitable place for luggage in the guest bedroom is important. This prevents suitcases ending up on the bed, bringing with them dust or dirt from outside.

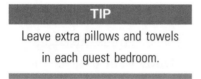

TIP

Leave extra pillows and towels in each guest bedroom.

You will need to supply electric blankets during the colder months. You need two pillows per person. You need at least two sets of bed linen per bed – more if you don't want to wash every day.

Think seriously about domestic linen if you are a larger Bed & Breakfast. It won't be able to withstand the daily washes and will fade very quickly.

Normal household bed sheets have an average life expectancy of 300 washes as against those used in hospitality able to last for 500 washes – they tend to be 50% polyester and 50% cotton. There are a number of linen suppliers to the hospitality industry. Look them up in the telephone directory. Ensure that you have spares of everything (blankets, pillows, sheets) in a cupboard in the guest room in case the guest's preference is for something different from the bedding provided. It is important to have a sheet and a light blanket as an alternative to a continental quilt. Many guests find even light quilts too hot.

When it comes to décor it needs to be neither too feminine nor too masculine. What it cannot be is childlike. You hear 'horror' stories from guests who have gone to a Bed & Breakfast only to find themselves sleeping with pictures of fairies, and 'Miranda's Room' on the door. Guests want to feel that the room they are staying in is theirs for the duration, so unless their name is Miranda and they are eight years old this room won't achieve it for them.

Floors should be carpeted or have rugs to help absorb noise and keep the room warmer in winter. It is very important that your window coverings, whether they are curtains or blinds, give total darkness in daylight. Your guests will probably want to sleep in and you need to ensure they can do so with ease.

You need bedside lights on both sides of the bed and plenty of accessible power points to cater for everything people travel with. Don't hide power points under the bed or behind furniture. What you don't want is double adaptors – they are extremely dangerous (see Chapter 9). All guest bedrooms should have a source of heating, with clear directions if needed.

Guest bedrooms must have locks on their doors. If your guests are staying for more than one night then they will want to keep personal effects in their room. They may feel they can't if there is no lock on the door and other guests can have access their space.

As for furniture, the most important piece, other than a bed, is a wardrobe – for those of you without fitted robes.

TIP
Some B&Bs have a small table and chairs for two in the guest bedrooms.

You should supply at least five, good quality hangers per guest, definitely not the bent-wire variety.

Bedside tables are important, with a tallboy or shelves for folded items. We would recommend a chair, and a desk is often appreciated – pens and notepaper are a nice addition. Don't forget the waste paper basket in every room. An adequate mirror is also essential.

When it comes to extras – think of everything you would like in the perfect bedroom and try to provide it. A jug and glasses is always appreciated. Mints are good. Tissues are essential.

> **TIP**
>
> A chocolate on your guest pillows is a nice touch.

Candles are a good idea – a great way to help create a romantic mood. Mini-CD players are also appreciated. If you wanted to go all out you could provide guest robes, a must when guests have to go out of their room to access the bathroom. Some people also appreciate facilities to make their own coffee and tea in their room.

HOME OFFICE

It is a good idea to set up a **home office.** You will need a space where you can do your paperwork, set up your computer, a facsimile and any other equipment you might need. The tax system requires you to keep precise records of your business activities and it is a good idea to have a dedicated room in which to do this. Your financial consultant will be able to advise whether or not there is a tax benefit here, it is likely there will be.

> **TIP**
>
> Have a list of items that are available for guests who may have left theirs at home. For example, toothbrush, toothpaste, nail file, comb, and aspirin, etc., for purchase if necessary or to just give them on request.

How and where you set this up is a personal choice. We suggest that you do not put this equipment in your bedroom. Your B&B will invade much of your personal space and you need one room in your house that is exempt from work.

BUILDING AND DEVELOPMENT APPLICATIONS

Before authorities adopt a code or policy it usually goes through a process of community exposure and consultation. The trouble here is that most people show little interest in these things until their proposed plan is directly affected. It's always better to obtain all the information and satisfy requirements to begin with.

Approval has traditionally been granted to operate a home occupation (yourself) or a home industry (where you might employ other people). In granting this approval authorities would again consider local amenity issues. For example, would it be noisy, have a lot of traffic coming and going, or incur other nuisance or environmental issues. Of course there are some informal, unapproved operations in existence, which authorities might not actively pursue unless they get a complaint about them.

APPROVAL AND CONSTRUCTION OF B&B ACCOMMODATION

The most daunting part of starting a B&B might be dealing with your local authority. It sounds pretty simple to set aside a couple of bedrooms, advertise in the local paper and in roll the customers. But don't forget that you will probably need the approval of the local authorities before you start operations. Otherwise an officer may knock on your door and ask for an explanation.

Dealing with your **local authority** can either be like talking with a close friend, or your worst nightmare realised. A combination of official zeal and ignorance can make the whole process confusing and frustrating. Suddenly the seemingly simple can become very complicated.

Usually, you will need to obtain **planning approval** for the use of the premises as a B&B plus building approval if any structural alterations or other modifications to the building are necessary. The good news is that usually you can make a combined application for both planning and building approval, which should speed up the process. In some instances the approvals, and certainly the building component, can be obtained through a private certifier.

A lot of the codes and policies are now written in a performance format, which means that authorities give you a series of objectives and some suggested ways of meeting those objectives. You have the flexibility to decide what you will do to achieve the requirements. However, you may still encounter some prescriptive requirements which simply state what you must do. While this format removes any doubts about getting it right, it also takes away some of the opportunity for flexibility and innovation.

Sometimes you will be hard pressed persuading authorities of the merits of your vision for your individual establishment, particularly if it deviates in some way from the rules that have been set down. Appeal rights against an authority's decision may vary and become so costly and time consuming to make your proposal not viable. It would be much better to negotiate as much as possible in the initial stages.

Be aware that different parts of a building can have different classifications depending on the use of the individual parts. This can have important implications for the final classification of a building and the required type of construction.

FIRE SAFETY

A new Fire Safety Order to apply in England and Wales (Northern Ireland and Scotland to have their own laws) will come into being on or about October 2006. The new Order will cover general fire precautions and fire safety duties that are needed to protect guests in case of fire. A set of guidance notes (not avaliable at the time of writing) will be available in advance of the changes coming into force. The guides will tell you what you have to do to comply with fire safety law, assistance in carrying out a fire risk assessment and identifing the general fire precautions you need to have in place.

If you have a query or require further information, then contact the Fire Safety Reform Team – email to fire.safetyreform@odpm. gov.uk For information on the Regulatory Review (Fire Safety) Order seminars, contact Cpd@abe.org.uk

At the very least, you would be required to install a system of hard-wired **smoke alarms** in every guest bedroom and in hallways associated with guest bedrooms. If there is no hallway, smoke alarms would need to be installed in areas between guest bedrooms and the remainder of the building, and between each storey. The smoke alarms in hallways and areas outside of guest bedrooms will also need to incorporate a light to be activated by the smoke alarm. Alternatively the smoke alarms can be wired to activate existing hallway lighting to assist evacuation of the occupants in the event of a fire.

In essence, the building must strictly adhere to all fire regulations with fire doors, fire extinguishers, smoke alarms and fire points. Bedroom windows must be all designed to act as emergency exits. It's also a good idea to have the fire alarm connected directly to the local fire station.

Fire blankets should be of a size to meet the expected risk. Your local fire service, fire authority or specialist fire-fighting supply and installation companies should guide you in your selection and installation of both fire extinguishers and fire blankets. If you are required to provide fire safety measures and facilities, such as smoke alarms, evacuation lighting, portable fire extinguishers and fire blankets, there will be regular inspections to verify that these measures are in place, are being maintained and are capable of operation at an acceptable standard that will afford occupants of the building the required level of fire safety. It currently is, and will be for the future, a requirement of the fire authority, and certainly in your own interest to limit liability, to have fire safety measures inspected by an appropriately qualified person who can certify that the fire safety measures are capable of working properly.

Depending on the nature, extent and location of any additions or alterations that you might want to carry out on your building, the authority may also require you to upgrade the fire protection between your building, any associated structures on your land and adjoining properties. This will depend on the existing and proposed separation between the buildings and property boundaries.

Of necessity, this information is of a general nature only and may not be directly applicable to individual circumstances, in which case individuals should seek expert advice. Prospective Bed & Breakfasts will need to check the new legislation and its application at the time of any proposed development. Existing B&Bs will, by law, be expected to comply with the pending new legislation.

ENERGY AND THE BED & BREAKFAST

If you need to build extra accommodation for your B&B or guest house, the following points need to be carefully considered. There is usually little additional cost for energy efficient alterations, but the resulting improvements in running costs and comfort are well worth the effort.

The climate in the United Kingdom, Ireland, the Channel Islands and the Isle of Man can vary quite considerably and often very swiftly.

In winter, with the sun predominantly in the southern sky, the longest wall of the house should face towards the south to receive the maximum exposure to the winter sunshine, providing free winter heat. Allowing natural light into your home instead of turning on lights cuts running costs considerably. In summer some shading may be required so that furniture is not damaged and curtains do not fade.

To make the most of the free heat, the rooms that require the most comfort should be located on the southern side of the home. These include the kitchen, play room, sitting room, dining room and any other room where comfort is needed during waking hours, for example, guest rooms without the use of a sitting room. Other rooms that do not require as much comfort during this time can be located on the north or east, for example, most bedrooms and spare rooms.

Consider the location of anything that could obstruct the winter sun from entering the home. This could include trees, neighbouring buildings or hills. Opportunities for winter sun entry to the new home or new additions need to be maximised.

Open plan designs might look good, but can create many problems. The house should be designed with zones that can be closed off from each other. This is mainly to reduce the extent of heating, but will give an added advantage of providing both visual and noise privacy. Staircases are notorious for causing difficulty with heating and need to have doors to separate them from heated areas. An airlock entry has two sets of doors in the foyer, the outer doors and a second inner set about 2 metres apart. This will allow entry to the home without allowing large amounts of heat to be lost in winter.

Triple-glazing and other improved forms of glazing can reduce conductive heat flow by more than 50%.

Internal building materials with high thermal mass can store large amounts of heat without causing a rapid temperature change throughout the day. These materials include a concrete slab on the ground, internal walls of brick, stone, concrete block, mud brick or rammed earth. By adding thermal mass into the south-facing living areas, the home can be kept warmer in winter, therefore reducing the amount of additional heating required.

Heat is lost or gained through five main areas in the house: the roof and ceilings, walls, windows and floors and also through draughts. To maintain comfort within the building, insulation should be used to control heat flows through each of these five areas. To insulate only one or two of these areas will not solve comfort problems. House design and construction are prescriptive to allow for maximum heat retention. The amount of insulation required for each locality is mentioned on the web site: www.est.org.uk.

Draughtproofing the house is one of the simplest and cheapest methods of improving comfort throughout the year. In older houses draughts are very common under and around doors, window frames, between floor boards, between floors and walls and skirting boards, wall and ceiling ventilators, recessed down lights, chimneys without dampers, and exhaust fans without dampers, etc. By filling the gaps, less hot air will flow out of the home.

There are many other topics of energy saving that need to be addressed. These include:

* the use of compact fluorescent lamps and fittings
* insulation of hot water pipes
* reduced lengths of hot water pipes
* efficient water heaters
* low water use appliances such as showerheads, washing machines, dishwashers, WC
* heat recovery on ventilation systems
* use of efficient white goods such as refrigerators, freezers, washing machines, clothes dryers

◆ energy-rated electronic equipment such as TV, video recorders, computers, printers and fax machines.

WHAT TO ASK YOUR ARCHITECT, BUILDER OR DESIGNER

If you are interested in having an energy efficient home, you should put the following questions to your architect, builder or designer.

◆ Does the house face south?
◆ Are the largest windows located on the southern side of the house?
◆ Is the appropriate level of insulation provided in the roof, the ceiling and all external walls?
◆ Can the living area be divided into separate zones, and have doors that can be closed to isolate those heated zones in the house?
◆ Is the hot water system located with the shortest pipe run to all facilities?
◆ What type of lighting will be provided in the house?

ADVICE FOR THE HOME RENOVATOR

The basic structure of your property will determine whether it is viable to renovate or not. If the house has deteriorated in the worst sense then you could be faced with rebuilding the house entirely and the cost of doing so is seldom reflected in the market value of the improved property.

If your house has already been renovated, unless your vision contains only minor changes, it can be very costly to undo someone else's work. It is often easier and less costly to start with a blank canvas. Renovating requires almost a Zen-like philosophy – you require patience, adaptability and a good sense of humour to endure the ongoing chaos. Keep the dream alive, the inspiration flowing, and the lines of communication wide open. And practise the art of compromise!

TIP

If the cost of renovating your property results in a market price over and above the reasonable value of similar properties in your area, then it probably isn't worthwhile.

WHEN YOU ARE THINKING OF RENOVATING

1. View your house as four walls and a roof, taking it back to the bare structure. Look at what you do and don't have. Look at ways to enhance what you have to achieve what you want, before using demolition tactics. It may save you a fortune in the long run. Be flexible with your ideas.

2. Look around your area for houses similar to that which you would like, taking note of market value. Will it be cheaper to build elsewhere, or buy a cheaper property to renovate? Even if you are looking at a long-term investment, it is important to stay focused on market value.

3. Ask yourself what effect you are hoping to create: olde worlde, modern, rustic, oriental, practical or luxurious are just a few examples. Do your existing windows, ceiling height and any other things that cannot be changed lend themselves to this particular idea?

4. Will the furniture that you need to buy to create the finished effect fit into the room? You would be surprised how many people have ordered furniture that will not go through their doorways.

5. You must be able to see the potential of the property. Some people are better at this than others, but there are ways to

learn. There is no point in listening to someone else convincing you of potential if you can't see it yourself.

6. Consult a professional before you purchase, or before you make the decision to renovate. Speak to an architect or builder, or even someone you know as a seasoned renovator, to get an understanding of the achievable and possible, and what it will cost to arrive at your dream. Unless you have a sound understanding of housing structure, get a qualified building inspection done, and include this as a condition of purchase.

7. Balance your renovations between personal requirements and general market appeal. Over specialising your property will narrow your resale market considerably.

8. Consider the layout of the house. It is much easier and cheaper to embellish the original layout of the house than to completely re-invent the entire house.

9. Remember the most expensive part of any renovation is the labour content. The more work you can do yourself the cheaper your renovation will be.

10. ▓ Be realistic – set yourself a timeframe, and then double it. This applies to using contractors, and more so to the do-it-yourself (DIY) renovator. A 'simple' job seldom is, and untold catastrophes can occur. Furthermore the constraints of full-time work, raising a family and social commitments can see your time allocated for renovating ebb and flow – so too your enthusiasm.

Be careful what building company you use. Always get more than one tradesperson to advise and quote you for the work required.

If the work you are having carried out is on a large scale then you should consult a surveyor. Remember, you may need planning permission for some renovations. However, if you have just moved into your home you should already have had a structural survey done.

Take into consideration that some renovations may require planning permission and may have to satisfy building regulations, for example; a new roof covering. The planning department of your local council should be able to advise you.

TIP

Before painting a complete room use a tester tin. Paint a patch on different walls, as each will reflect the colour differently.

PLANNING PERMISSION

How much you can extend the dwelling will depend on your local authority and their individual policy. It also depends on the property type you wish to alter. There can be different limits on bungalows, semi-detached, detached, end-of-terrace and terraced properties.

There is not always a need to gain **planning permission** as some extension work and loft conversions can be done under **Permitted Development**. This allows you to build a certain amount without submitting plans. Each government or local authority has a different, and definite, policy on what meterage is acceptable.

If you don't need to get planning permission, then a **certificate of lawful development** can be issued to you. It will show that you have submitted plans and that you were legally allowed to carry out the works.

TIP

It is a good idea to occasionally spend the night in one of your guest rooms, testing the room's appeal, the condition of the bed and your bathroom facilities. This will help you gauge the service you are offering.

If you are building a garage then planning permission is not always needed. Once again each authority has its own policy on meterage and siting. The roof of the garage also needs to be taken into consideration, as there are different policies for pitched and flat roofs. Permitted Development is not available on all properties, such as a listed building, a building near a conservation area, or new housing developments. These will all have their own set of policies.

5

Doing Your Homework

O ver the past few years, when speaking to thousands of
prospective Bed & Breakfast owners, we have often faced the
dilemma of how to sound enthusiastic about people's prospective
ventures, while still issuing a word of caution.

To many people, more than any other venture, owning and
operating a Bed & Breakfast represents a romantic ideal. We see
normally rational people – doctors, lawyers, business owners,
teachers, policemen, process workers – about to take huge
financial risks on a venture for which they have not written a
feasibility study.

No matter what your financial or personal expectations for your
new venture, it is a business and you need to treat it with the
gravity it deserves. You will find it impossible to achieve the
results you want without a blueprint on how you plan to get
there.

In this chapter we aim to give you some advice that you may find
helpful to get you started in your venture.

SCOUT'S HONOUR

If there was one piece of advice that we would give you it is to: **be prepared**.

More businesses fail due to lack of planning and ongoing financial management than for any other reason.

So why don't people plan to succeed? The main reason cited is time, or the lack of it. *Make time*. This is your life or livelihood we are talking about. A few extra months planning your venture, researching the business you are thinking of entering, *will* make the difference between success and failure.

Get out the notebook we talked about in the first chapter and write down your answers to the following questions:

- Do you have any business experience? Write down how you believe you can use this experience in your business.

- Do you have any other experiences you can draw on? How do you believe they will help you?

- Have you spoken to an accountant, financial adviser or business consultant?

- Have you contacted your region's tourism office to get information on your area's tourism statistics? Ask them for the number of B&Bs in your area.

- Have you contacted your local authority to get their position on Bed & Breakfast?

- Have you spoken to at least five other operators about their B&B experience?

◆ Have you stayed in at least five Bed & Breakfasts? This is important so that you can test the adequacy of the bedroom, specifically the bed, and the bathroom against your perceptions. Write down things you believe these B&Bs are doing well, and the things you believe they could improve on. Ensure your plan addresses these issues.

◆ Why do you believe there is a demand for another Bed & Breakfast in your area? What will be your main advantage over your competitors?

◆ Have you spoken to your area's Bed & Breakfast association if there is one? Have you contacted the national office?

◆ Is your Bed & Breakfast to be a life-style change or a commercial venture in the stand-alone sense?

◆ Are you buying an existing business? Have you contacted your financial or business adviser to help you assess the business? Have you had a building inspection?

◆ Have you determined the financial goals you have for the business?

◆ Have you discussed with your financial adviser or business consultant the effect of turning your house into a business will have on your financial affairs?

◆ Have you looked at various tourism and industry publications?

◆ Have you sought the opinions of potential customers and suppliers?

◆ Have you worked out how much it will cost you to turn your house into a Bed & Breakfast? Did you get three quotes for all work you are not going to do yourself?

◆ Have you worked out a financial plan to supplement your income while you build your business?

FINANCING

In the first year of your new enterprise you should try to **finance** your venture yourself. However, if additional funding is necessary you need to ensure you contact your small business association or consultant, your bank or building society, or a financial adviser. Remember, all start-up businesses need initial seed capital and Bed & Breakfast is not an exception.

You need to take the answers of all the questions above to any meetings you have regarding finance. It will show you have done your preparation and will keep you focused.

STARTING YOUR OWN BED & BREAKFAST

So why start your Bed & Breakfast from scratch rather than buy an existing business?

Firstly, you are not paying for goodwill or that intangible stamp the current owners have put on the property. The value of the property is one thing, the individual characteristic, if proven, is something else. Both aspects are treated separately.

Any reputation an establishment has, is the reputation it has earned. If selling or buying an existing Bed & Breakfast, remember that the B&B or guest house name, attached to the property, can be part of the sale or purchase, or a point of negotiation.

You don't need to spend a lot of money at once. Your capital outlay can be gradual. You avoid the exit and entry costs of selling and buying a property. You will have the satisfaction of building the business from an embryo to a living, breathing thing.

However, starting a Bed & Breakfast from scratch is not all beer and skittles. You will have all the set up tasks associated with starting a Bed & Breakfast, finding good suppliers, buying beds, dealing with contractors, etc. You will need to work in conjunction with your tourist association to build a relationship. You will need to live off your savings or paying job until people hear about you.

BUYING AN ESTABLISHED B & B

Am I saying that buying an established Bed & Breakfast is better? No, just different. The advantages are as follows:

(a) There is no start-up period.

(b) If you are a good operator with a solid business you could have a substantial positive cash flow from the word go.

A marketing strategy is already in place. Your business should already be listed in your area's tourism book and a nationally recognised B&B guide so that you have a place in two popular Bed & Breakfast guides for your region.

If purchasing, your predecessors already have an identifiable target market. This does not mean you can't change it over time, but for now you have a ready and, hopefully, willing clientele.

Most of the establishment decisions have been made – as you have purchased the property we will take it for granted that you believe the decisions were the right ones. That leaves you to get on with the business of the day to day running of the establishment.

Are there disadvantages? Certainly.

You will be investing a large amount of capital immediately. If this is to be your career then that is not such a problem, if it's just a way to earn some extra cash, then the financial commitment could be far too large.

You could be paying too much for your prospective business. You need to determine how important the previous owner was to the business, how much return business you can expect when considering the purchase price. Look at the visitor's book and assess how much the business could potentially suffer during the changeover period.

You will be tying up your funds in a business that takes time to sell, if the need arises. You will be paying more than if it were just a family home. Be aware of this before making any decisions.

You need to assess whether what you are paying for the furniture, en suites, china, etc. is a reasonable price.

A copy of the audited tax returns for last thee years will be required to enable your accountant to better advise you on the viability of the business for sale and how much is it really worth.

If you chose to buy an existing B&B then remember that you are making two decisions:

1. A property decision.
2. A business decision.

You must know how much the vendor wants for the property as against how much for the business. If you understand this, you are on the way in making a better commercial decision.

IS IT GOING TO WORK?

In order to make sense of all the above you need to first test the viability of your proposed B&B investment by completing a **feasibility study** – see next chapter. It is important to remember, however, that knowledge is not an end in itself. You must use the knowledge gained from completing this feasibility study as your worksheet and stepping-stone to achieving your goals and aspirations.

The main message is that the research you need to do to make your B&B a success must be unique to you and your market. If the findings in your feasibility study are positive then the assumptions can be used as a basis for your business plan. It can also be used as a confidential worksheet for your own personal use and so propel you to the next level of commitment. On the other hand, if the results of your study are negative, then move on.

6

Doing Your Feasibility Study

I n discussion with my colleague Wal Reynolds we formulated a method of assessing whether your proposal is viable. This becomes your feasibility study.

No matter how you view it, your Bed & Breakfast venture is a proposed business. People go into business for many different reasons, e.g. independence, status, lifestyle, boredom or whatever.

The key and overriding reason for going into business is to make money. If you don't make money you can't stay in business – it's as simple as that. All the other reasons quoted above are secondary.

It is well known that small businesses fail at an alarming rate, but what is not so well known is that most of these failures could have been avoided. There are two key reasons for failure:

1. The people themselves.
2. Poor management.

Many people are not suited to going into business. They may be deficient in people skills or lack the discipline necessary to run a business, or they are unable to cope with change, pressure, problem solving, etc. They may also not be physically equipped for the demands of the business, or far more commonly, they do not have the back up and support of their partners and/or family.

ISSUE ANALYSIS

We are constantly amazed at just how many people have the idea, sometime or other, of going into his or her own Bed & Breakfast business. On the surface it looks a really attractive proposition, with plenty of positives and very few negatives. Closer examination, however, gives a different story. The number of people who have the original idea and then reject it, is high.

This next section assumes that **you and your family** have already decided that **you** are suitable people to be in the Bed & Breakfast industry.

The discussion period

Once the idea has been formed, it is usual to have discussion on the proposal and its implications. There is usually very little detail or information at this stage, and a high percentage of the ideas die due to an unwillingness or inability to proceed further.

The first assessment

The first assessment is a period where information is gathered on key facts such as location, costs, staff requirements, time constraints and a whole host of operating details. A lot of potential Bed & Breakfast operators lose their motivation or interest at this point as they begin to realise just how much investment is needed in the form of planning, time, money and effort.

The research period

At this stage, potential B&B operators need answers, i.e. facts and details upon which they can build a comprehensive picture of their proposed operation, the possible market, the methods of operation, etc. They need to undertake research to give them a realistic understanding of their proposed business. Again, many more potential B&B operators drop out as their research shows their idea to be either impractical, non-viable, too complicated or very commonly, a resultant picture totally different from what was originally expected.

The appreciation of commitment

After conducting the initial research, there is a clearer picture of the commitment that has to be made with regard to time, money, assets and labour required to get the Bed & Breakfast up and running. Many people decide at this stage that starting a Bed & Breakfast is not what they really want to do.

Poor management

While approximately 50% of small business failure can be traced to people who were not suited to going into business, a further 40% of failures can be directly traced to poor management, e.g. lack of planning, or poor planning, lack of finance (both start up and working capital), incorrect management style, lack of experience and/or training, poor time management, and surprisingly, poor selection and use of professional support.

It is in this area of poor management that most failures can be easily avoided. Good management begins with good planning – and good planning must have accurate information upon which decisions can be made.

YOUR PLANNING

The planning that you need to undertake at this stage of your thinking is not, surprisingly, what is commonly referred to as a business plan. You cannot have a business plan if you don't have a business!

What you should be considering is 'what planning must I do to put my business idea into practice?' You also need to evaluate the viability or otherwise of your proposed Bed & Breakfast.

You are, in reality, looking at putting together a feasibility study. The depth and direction of this feasibility study will depend upon the type of B&B you are proposing. Are you looking at a stand-alone commercial venture, or are you considering a life-style adjustment by using your existing dwelling?

Stand-alone commercial venture

It is deemed to be a commercial venture when you construct a building specifically designed as a B&B or acquiring a property and converting it to a B&B. In this case, your study will look at your capital needs and potential returns from the following options.

The options are:

1. To purchase land, construct and fit out the building and grounds, with provision of enough working capital to survive the first three to six months.

2. To purchase an existing property, modify it to meet your plans and standards, plus once again, sufficient working capital for the first three to six months.

3. To convert your existing dwelling into a dedicated B&B operation.

In point 3, you are looking at investing your land and buildings (your dwelling) into the business and as such you must look at it as the equivalent of a cash injection. You will need capital to modify your property and you will also need working capital.

In all the above options you are looking at starting a business in a highly competitive market and are assuming the risks that any business owner must face. You will need good management skills as well as capital to make your business succeed. We suggest that you start by writing your own feasibility study.

If you have to source finance for your proposal, the feasibility study is critical to provide your potential lenders with the information they need. If you are fortunate enough to have sufficient capital available, then the feasibility study will provide you with the viability evaluation and assurance that you will require before investing.

A life-style adjustment
This is when you decide to convert part of your existing dwelling into a B&B operation as a means of generating a secondary income. This may well become a source of prime income in the future.

This type of operation is quite common and our research has shown that the main groups to consider this path are:

◆ Couples who wish to take advantage of an 'empty nest' as a result of their children leaving home.

◆ People who have lost their partner and want to stay active and have people around.

◆ Retirees on fixed incomes, especially 'baby boomers'.

The common thread is that these people are looking at what may be described as 'topping up' income, that is, income to supplement other existing sources, rather than a stand-alone income as described in the dedicated business B&B group.

The feasibility model we are providing is applicable to both groups, that is, the stand-alone commercial venture and the life-style change projects.

The depth of detail you will need to provide for this study depends upon which group you fall into. If it is the life-style adjustment group, some parts of the study model will be irrelevant and your financial analysis will also change slightly. The core elements, however, will be just as critical to both groups.

The direction of your feasibility study will be determined by your answers to three very direct and personal questions.

1. Do you have your family support?
2. Are you prepared to adopt B&B as a way of life?
3. Do you know what you want in your personal life?

If you have a family, their support is essential to your success.

Should your partner and family not be equally committed, then you could find yourself stretched, isolated and at many times lacking critical support, whether in the form of back-up, access to family assets or even just someone with whom you can talk. Remember that you are asking your family to make sacrifices for the business and that you will be changing their way of life. Don't assume that they will support you – involve them and ask for their support.

A fact – operating a Bed & Breakfast is not just a 9 to 5 job.

It is easy to see that your role as host demands long hours. Uninterrupted weekends, as you may know them now, will disappear and the luxury of a private life-style will probably be non-existent, especially in the early stage.

To be successful your life will revolve around the demands of the Bed & Breakfast operation and your guests. Are you prepared to accept this?

Finally, one of the greatest causes of stress in owning your own business is having a conflict between what you want to do in your private life and what you have to do in your business life. No business is worth a marriage break-up or serious health problems. Your business is the vehicle to provide you with the means of achieving what you want to do in your private life.

Therefore it is important that you sit down and visualise exactly what you would like to achieve both personally and with your family. What private projects do you want to complete? What personal milestones do you want to achieve and how do you want to allocate your time?

We all have wish lists for such things as hobbies, holidays, acquisitions and investments, as well as prior commitments that we must keep.

It is only when these personal priorities are written down with a time frame for achievement that you will be able to foresee possible conflicts between your private life and your proposed business demands.

WRITING YOUR FEASIBILITY STUDY

Someone once said that every dream must have the structure of a plan. The saying that you get what you plan for is very true. Your dream won't just happen. You need to develop a strategy to achieve that dream.

Creating a 'feasibility study' for your dream is a practical starting point where you work through all the key areas you need to consider. As we stated earlier, a feasibility study is an exercise to assist you in making your investment decisions. It is also a formalised analysis that can encourage meaningful discussions with your partners, family advisers and potential lenders.

When you write it, use your own language and your own writing style. To give your study some organisation, and to make it easier to write and read, adopt a structure for your layout and presentation.

Your study should contain the following sections which you can adapt as you see fit.

Cover sheet
Contents list
1. Your business idea
2. Your professional support
3. Your target market
   3.1 Location
   3.2 Your premises
   3.3 Your real estate decisions
   3.4 Operational issues
4. Your financial analysis
   4.1 Desired income
   4.2 Capital requirements
   4.3 Financial viability
5. Your decision
Appendices

Let's now look at each of these items in more detail.

Your cover sheet is designed to identify your study and to display a confidentiality warning to prevent or deter any unauthorised reading.

Your contents page is simply an index of the contents of your study. It is an organisational tool to facilitate easy reading of your study.

Your business idea
This written outline of your business idea is designed to help you focus more clearly on what exactly you are planning in your B&B operation. How would you describe your idea to someone else? Why will your proposal be different from other B&B operations? Why should people want to stay with you? What will you offer

them, apart from somewhere to stay? In short, why will your Bed & Breakfast operation be successful? This one-page summary is not easy to write so don't be surprised if you re-write it many times. However, the clearer you express your Bed & Breakfast idea on paper, the easier it will be to achieve in practice.

Your professional support
The success of any business operation can be directly linked to accessing quality professional support. You will need key advisers and mentors to assist you in formulating your ideas, guiding your progress, and watching over you and giving you not only feedback, but most importantly, someone to talk to. Your professional team should comprise:

◆ your accountant or financial adviser
◆ your solicitor
◆ your banker
◆ your insurance agent/broker
◆ your B&B association representative
◆ your business mentor or paid adviser.

Your accountant should be one of your key advisers, not just someone who does your tax returns. You should consider using your accountant to guide you in such areas as:

◆ your preferred legal structure (sole trader, partnership, company, trust)
◆ your financial and funding options
◆ your approach to your financial source
◆ your books and control systems
◆ your taxation requirements, registrations and returns including VAT returns where applicable, capital gains, etc.

- your financial reporting and forecasts
- your superannuation options.

We suggest you look around for an accountant who you can relate to: someone who can speak your language, answer your questions and most importantly, someone not too busy to return your calls and give you help and advice *when* you need it.

Your solicitor should be used to check any contract, especially leases, before you sign them. We are, whether we like it or not, living in an age of litigation and the best legal insurance you can arrange is to have a good solicitor. You should also use your solicitor to assist you when you construct your own legal checklist.

The banking industry is changing daily and it is unlikely that you will have access to a bank manager. You will probably be dealing with a lending or a relationship officer who will be charged with looking after your account. Try to foster a relationship with your contact person, but before you reach this stage, have a good look around to see which bank is the best for you and your needs.

As far as **insurance** is concerned, remember that it is a highly competitive market, and you should not be just shopping for the best price. We suggest that you should look at obtaining at least three quotes before you sign up. We also suggest that you check with your local tourism authority and/or other B&B operators to obtain the names of the insurance companies they use and are prepared to recommend.

Your B&B association/tourism authority will provide you with the industry support, networking and the back up you will require if you want to succeed in the industry. Being a member gives access to market research, industry news, training, workshops and best practices by networking with others in the industry.

Having a good **business mentor** or a paid adviser is only now being recognised as one of the keys to business success. A business mentor is simply someone with knowledge and empathy who is available to act as a coach, a guide, a motivator and a sounding board. He or she is someone who can discuss your business and management ideas with you and help you make informed and effective decisions. Your mentor need not be someone totally specialising in the B&B industry. He or she should be, however, someone with business experience who can pass on advice, opinions and information to help make you a better manager.

Your target market

Remember that your B&B will not appeal to everybody and that you should be identifying the type of guests you want to attract, i.e. your preferred target market.

What type of guests would you like to attract to your B&B? The choice is yours – you should at this early stage make this decision. Would you prefer to be servicing the top of the market or the no-frills sector? Would you feel more comfortable with corporate clients or with family groups? Your choice of target market will be a vital factor in influencing your decision on where to locate and how to design your premises. If, on the other hand, you decide to use your existing dwelling with modifications, then you must determine what type of guest your Bed & Breakfast will attract.

The following table contains ten categories of target guests to help you to identify your prime market group and also your preference towards two subsidiary groups listed in order. Socio-economic considerations should apply in all categories, as should preferred age brackets.

Table 1 Target market options

Market segment	Prime market	Subsidiary market 1	Subsidiary market 2
Affluent guests			
Couples			
Singles			
Families			
Corporate			
Guests with a disability			
Budget market			
Groups			
Gay/lesbian			
Pets			
Other			

Note: Use one tick only in each column.

Having identified your preferred market groups (this also indicates age and income), you can now look at your location.

Your location

When deciding where to establish your proposed B&B, we suggest that you and your family choose three regions that appeal to you and where you could all comfortably live. Be sure that they are all inside a four-hour driving range from a metropolitan area (where the bulk of the population is) and/or on a major link road to somewhere.

These three selections are:

Region 1 ....

Region 2 ....

Region 3 ....

These three regions can now be researched for the following information:

Local government policy
In each of the three regions contact the local shire or city council town planning officer and ask for a run-down on all tourist related development conducted in the region during the last five years. Find out what is planned for the future. Another question to ask is what is the council's attitude towards fostering tourism in general and B&B in particular. They may have a policy document on B&B operations that you could obtain, or the information may be available from their web page.

Regional tourism
Visit each region's tourism office and ask them whether they think they are getting their share of the applicable county and region tourist pound/euro. If not, then why not?

Ask them for a copy of their current tourism growth figures and the projected ones as well. Also, find out the demographics of those tourists who visit the region and where they live. In all probability, you will find there is a predominant area. You need this information in order to determine whether or not your target market groups come into the area in reasonable numbers.

Find out how many Bed & Breakfasts are in the region, what markets they target and are servicing. Most tourist offices have access to market research on travel patterns in each area and this information is available and surprisingly detailed.

Visit the region's Chamber of Commerce and ask where they think the region will be in economic terms in the foreseeable future.

It is also a good idea to visit some real estate offices to find out how the local property market is faring. This will give you an idea on property prices, availability and trends.

Your regional assessment
At this point we assume that you have personally visited all three regions and have the salient information to evaluate your findings by completing the following table.

Table 2 Regional options

Information gained on:	Region 1	Region 2	Region 3
Past tourism development			
Future tourism development			
Attitude towards tourism			
Attitude towards B&B			
Policy on P&B			
Development attractions			
Average length of stay			
Number of tourists p.a.			

Note: Place either a P or N beside each item: P = Positive, N = Negative

The information gathered when visiting the regional tourism offices, Chambers of Commerce, local government and estate agencies should now be marked in the table below, again by placing either a P or N beside each question in the applicable column.

Table 3 Regional status

Information gained on:	Region 1	Region 2	Region 3
Regional share of the tourist pound/euro			
Current tourism			
Growth statistics			
Future tourism projections			
Visitor demographics			
Point of visitor origin			
Number of B&Bs			
B&B markets			
Chamber of Commerce findings			
Real estate values			

Having completed the above exercise you will probably find that one region in particular stands out from the rest. Through this process of elimination, you have identified the region that is developing for:

◆ tourism growth
◆ sound and reasonable local government B&B policy
◆ innovative tourist association activity
◆ your target markets coming into the region in acceptable numbers
◆ real estate values that are within your budget.

In essence, you now have meaningful commercial knowledge about the region you have nominated in which to establish both your family and your B&B business. Let us now look at your proposed Bed & Breakfast premises.

Your B&B premises

Having meaningful commercial knowledge about your selected region, you can now set about planning the floor area of the dwelling that is going to house your family and guests.

Whatever your prime and subsidiary markets are, be sure that you plan the floor layout in such a way that it matches your guests' requirements. Remember, when people choose a Bed & Breakfast stay, they are often more discerning guests. It is also vital to configure the dwelling so that the family's living requirements do not conflict with those of the guests or vice versa. The following table will assist you when working out the facilities required for your potential guests.

Table 4 Facility options

Family facilities	Yes/No	Number
Bedrooms with en suites		
Bedrooms with shared bathroom		
Drawing/living rooms		
Semi-industrial kitchen		
Normal kitchen		
Pantry		
Garage		
Workshop		
Storage room		
Office		
Laundry		
Other (please specify)		
Dining room		

It is also vital to know what your family requirements are and we therefore suggest that you complete the following table that will assist you in itemising all the facilities required for your family.

Table 5 Family requirements

Family facilities	Yes/No	Number
Bedrooms with en suites		
Bedrooms with shared bathroom		
Drawing/living rooms		
Semi-industrial kitchen		
Normal kitchen		
Pantry		
Garage		
Workshop		
Storage room		
Office		
Laundry		
Other (please specify)		

The information from these two tables should allow you to draw up a floor plan for your proposed B&B.

Your real estate decisions

Once you have a floor plan drawn up, you can take it along to a carefully selected real estate agent and ask them whether they know of any property for sale that has a floor area similar to the one you are seeking or enough space to mould to your design. Check also that the location of any such property is ideal for both the guests and the family. If you cannot find a suitable property to adjust and craft into what you want, then you need to look for a block of land suitably positioned on which you can purpose-build your Bed & Breakfast.

Whatever the outcome, you will need to visit your local council's planning department in order to be aware of their building code and to ascertain whether there are any impediments that could be costly to overcome or impossible to consider. When you visit the local government planning department you will also be able to gain an estimate of their charges. These charges will relate to the lodging of your development application plus any other charges relating to your proposal.

Your start-up capital costs

Let us assume that you have followed our suggestions to date:

◆ you have identified your prime target market, let's say 'the more affluent guests'
◆ you have nominated your two subsidiary markets, let's say 'corporate' and 'singles'
◆ you have identified and researched three regions, and selected one
◆ you have drawn up a site plan that will suit your proposals and have checked this plan with the local government planning section
◆ you have looked at your real estate options and have found a property in the right location for you and your family and your guests, which can be adapted to your requirements.

Let us also assume that this property has a value or purchase price of £/€400,000.

The next stage is to work out just how much it will cost to put into place any alterations and improvements you want, together with the furnishings you require. We suggest you refer to your floor plan and construct a list of everything you can think of that you will require in your Bed & Breakfast.

The following table gives a hypothetical example of such a list, and enables you to identify the capital costs of purchasing items, and improvements as required for B&B purposes.

Table 6 Capital cost options

Items	Yes/No	Qty	£/€ Value
King-sized beds	N		0
Queen-sized beds	Y	4	4,500
Bedside tables	Y	8	1,200
Wardrobes	N		0
Carpets	Y	6	15,000
Curtains/blinds	Y	12	8,000
Other bedroom fittings	Y	4	1,000
Bathroom PC items	N		0
Lounge furniture	Y	3	9,000
Meeting room furniture	N		0
Electrical e.g. TVs, video	Y	5	5,000
Dining tables	Y	4	4,000
Office equipment	Y	N/A	5,000
Tennis court/equipment	Y	1	20,000
Swim pool/equipment	N		0
Outdoor furniture	Y	4	2,000
Bedding/linen	Y	6	5,500
Sundry/miscellaneous e.g. pot plants, etc	Y	N/A	1,500
Alterations to dwelling	Y		43,300
Total			**125,000**

The 'sundry' or 'miscellaneous' heading is for all the small and sundry items you will require, e.g. pot plants, umbrella stands, etc. In this example, the sundry item is around 1% of your total furnishing and dwelling alteration costs.

The other major start-up costs to be considered are your professional fees, e.g. your solicitor and accountant/financial adviser, plus any stamp duty required on the transaction.

Your set-up capital costs can now be determined as shown in the hypothetical example in the following table.

Table 7 Set-up amounts

Set-up capital costs	£/€
Purpose-built B&B	Nil
Existing property purchase	400,000
Alterations/improvements	125,000
Local government charges	2,000
Professional fees e.g. legal, accountancy	8,000
Stamp duty (if applicable)	6,500
Total	**541,500**

YOUR FINANCIAL VIABILITY

The easiest way to evaluate the financial viability of your proposed B&B is to focus on net profit. The reason for this is that you need net profit to pay for your living expenses and your loan repayments unless you have another source of income that will subsidise these payments.

In other words, whether your B&B is to be a stand-alone commercial venture or a life-style adjustment, you will need it to generate enough net profit to:

♦ allow you and your family to live
♦ repay your loan principal
♦ pay your associated taxes.

At this level of net profit, if all you can do is to pay for these three outlays above, then you are, at the best, just breaking even.

Net profit is usually found by the following rule:

Total trading income   £/€_____
Less cost of production   £/€_____
Equals gross profit   £/€_____
Less all operational costs   £/€_____
Equals net profit*   £/€_____

* Before tax and drawings

Your feasibility study should adopt net profit as its main viability indicator. This viability can be established in eight simple steps, as follows:

Step 1 Evaluate your personal net worth.
Step 2 Determine your funds/assets available for investment.
Step 3 Calculate your total investment needs and your borrowing totals.
Step 4 Calculate your real monthly living costs.
Step 5 Estimate your annual net profit requirements.
Step 6 Determine your required annual sales level.
Step 7 Establish the reality of your sales target.
Step 8 Make a decision.

Let us look at each step in detail and in so doing, continue with the hypothetical example we were using earlier.

Evaluate your personal net worth
Step 1. Your personal net worth is simply a listing of all your family's assets and liabilities. This is a standard starting procedure for any investment analysis.

In our hypothetical model, let us assume the following net worth.

Table 8 Personal net worth

Total value of all assets	£/€ 750,000
Total value of all liabilities	£/€ 150,000
Net worth (assets less liabilities)	£/€ **600,000**

Suggestion: Approach your own bank or financial institution and ask for a copy of their user-friendly worksheets. They all produce these to assist you with your net worth calculations.

Determine your total funds and assets available for investment
Step 2. From your list of assets in Step 1, determine which assets you are prepared to invest in your proposed venture, and total their value. Don't forget to include cash that may be available. These funds would also include any loans you may take out using items of property as security, e.g. a second mortgage. In the example we are using, let us assume that your equity funds available are £/€58,500.

Investment needs and your borrowing totals
Step 3. You will need funds for:

◆ set-up capital costs
◆ working capital requirements.

Your set-up capital costs were discussed earlier (see Table 7) where we estimated that our start-up capital costs, in our example, were £/€541,500.

In our hypothetical example we are assuming that the family home will be sold at a price which will enable purchase of the new B&B property, and cover the payment of local government charges, professional fees, etc. This means that we only need to fund £/€125,000 for alterations and improvements.

Working capital is the amount you require to run your B&B operation on a daily basis. You cannot assume that your B&B will produce income from day one, which means that you will need access to funds to pay for day-to-day operational expenses for the first three to six months. This may seem an excessive period, but you would be wise to check with your financial adviser on this issue. The following table will help you determine your level of working capital.

Table 9 Working capital – £/€

Item	Month 1	Month 2	Month 3	Second quarter	Total £/€
Operating expenses					
Accountancy					
Advertising					
Assoc. – Tourism B&B					
Bank charges					
Gardening, also pool					
Insurance					
Internet costs					
Laundry					
Postage					
Power					
Printing and stationery					
Repairs and maintenance					
Mortgage payments					
Telephone					
Travelling expenses					
Vehicle costs					
Wages and salaries					
Production cost					
Food and provisions					
Commissions on sales					
Cleaning					
Miscellaneous					
Total running costs	1,400	1,450	1,500	4,950	9,300
Add non-perishable purchases	50	55	60	210	375
Total £/€ value	1,450	1,505	1,560	5,160	9,675

In this example we have assumed a total working capital requirement of £/€9,675.

Formulate your own worksheet and use this information to estimate your borrowing needs.

Table 10 Borrowing needs

For assets needed (capital costs)	£/€125,000
For working capital required (first six months)	£/€9,675
Total funds needed	**£/€134,675**
Less equity funds available from step 2	£/€58,500
Total to be borrowed	**£/€76,175**

Calculate your living costs

Step 4. We stressed early in this book that your business is the means by which you are able to meet your family's lifestyle requirements and budgets. Table 11 is designed to assist you in arriving at a realistic summation of your own and your family's monthly living costs. You will notice that we have shown these costs in three categories, i.e. fixed, variable and discretionary.

Fixed costs are just that. There is no flexibility in either their amount or their required date of payment, e.g. loan repayments, council rates, car registrations, etc. Variable costs can be adjusted in relation to their amount or their date of payment. Examples in this group are clothing, food, maintenance, etc. Discretionary costs are those which you have total control as to whether or not you want to incur them, e.g. gifts, entertainment, holidays.

As we are aware, our living costs will vary from month to month, with some months being far more expensive than others. To get a realistic picture we suggest you look at your total year's activity and then work out an average monthly cost. For our assumed example, we are showing the following monthly livings costs as:

Table 11 Monthly living costs

Total fixed costs (e.g. rates, car registration etc)	£/€600
Total variable costs (e.g. food, petrol etc)	£/€1,500
Total discretionary costs (e.g. holidays, total savings)	£/€500
Total monthly living costs	£/€2,600

Armed with this information we can now move on to the next step.

Your annual net profit requirement
Step 5. The net profit you require must be enough to:

♦ pay for your personal drawings/wage equivalent
♦ provide you with a reasonable return on your equity investment.

Your level of drawings must be sufficient to pay for your monthly living costs. In the example we are using, we have established our average monthly living costs to be £/€2,600, that is, £/€31,200 per annum.

It is also standard practice to expect some return on the money you have invested in your B&B. (If you invested your funds into an external venture you would expect a return.) Let us assume for this example that a reasonable annual return is 8%. The profits you will need from your Bed & Breakfast will therefore, in this example, be:

1. Drawings of at least the level of your annual living costs (refer to Table 11) i.e. monthly costs of £/€2,600 × 12 = £/€31,200, plus

2. Return on invested equity (refer to Table 10) i.e. 8% on £/€58,500 = £/€4,680 **Total net profit needed £/€ 35,880**.

In the calculations so far, we have assumed your B&B to be a stand-alone commercial venture rather than a life-style adjustment. As a stand-alone commercial venture, the net profit figure of £/€35,880 is the minimum net profit you need just to break even. If, however, your Bed & Breakfast is not a stand-alone venture, and you have income from other sources, your net profit expectations could be much lower. If this is the case, we suggest you nominate the level of net profit you require to top up your other income sources.

Once you have established your net profit requirements, the next step is to look at the sales level required to provide you with this profit.

Establish your annual sales level
Step 6. In our viability exercise so far, we have focused on net profit and worked out how much net profit we require, in pounds/euros to break even. Once we have this net profit figure, we can work backwards to estimate the sales level required to produce this net profit.

Working in percentages as well as pounds/euros does this. Let us look once again at the net profit formula, this time with the idea of expressing all items as a percentage of trading income.

Table 12 Net profit analysis

	£/€	%
Total trading income	£/€	100
Less cost of production	£/€	25
Equals gross profit	£/€	75
Less operating expenses	£/€	50
Equals net profit (before tax and drawings)	£/€	25

It is our experience that costs of production, i.e. food and provisions can usually run around 25% of trading income.

Given this estimate, gross profit would represent 75% of trading income. From this 75% we have to deduct all operating expenses.

In a stand-alone commercial Bed & Breakfast enterprise, we believe that a minimum industry average of around 25% total income is an acceptable level of net profit. This percentage can be higher, contingent on occupancy levels, and whether or not you out-source tasks like cleaning etc. The more you do yourself the higher the net profit. If your Bed & Breakfast is a stand-alone commercial operation then we can assume in our example that:

1. net profit needed is £/€ 35,880, and
2. this net profit is say, 25% of total income.

Our required sales or trading income required would therefore be: £/€35,880 × 100/25 or £/€143,520 per annum.

If, however, your Bed & Breakfast proposal is a life-style adjustment rather than a stand-alone business, you will need to look at the top-up income you require to augment your other income.

If this top-up income is say, only £/€9,000 per annum, then your sales or trading income required from your B&B will be: £/€9,000 × 100/25 or £/€36,000 per annum.

Establish the reality of your sales target
Step 7. At this stage, ask the question: 'Can guest bookings at this level be reached?' To gain a more realistic appreciation of your yearly trading targets, look at this as a monthly or weekly figure:

Critical amounts – sales/trading targets

Table 13

Sales/trading targets	Stand-alone business	Life-style adjustments
Yearly sales target	£/€143,520	£/€36,000
Monthly sales target (12 months/year)	£/€11,960	£/€3,000
Weekly sales target (48 weeks/year)	£/€2,990	£/€750

The answers relate directly to:

1. The number of rooms available for guest use.
2. The room rates you will charge.
3. Your potential and likely occupancy rates.
4. Your marketing strategy and its effectiveness.

To help you in working out your ability to meet your target income levels, we suggest you construct a daily room rate income 'ready reckoner' similar to the following table:

Table 14 Room rates per night

Guest rooms	£/€120	£/€130	£/€140	£/€150	£/€170	£/€200
1	120	130	140	150	170	200
2	240	260	280	300	340	400
3	360	390	420	450	510	600
4	480	520	560	600	680	800
5	600	650	700	750	850	1000

This ready reckoner is a simple way of matching the room rates you select with the number of guest rooms available. However, it does not take into account your expected occupancy rate. The next table allows you to quickly convert your guest room availability and your expected occupancy rate into yearly-anticipated bed nights. We are working on a 48-week per year basis.

Table 15 Occupancy – yearly bed nights

Guest rooms	15%	25%	35%	50%	60%
1	50	84	118	168	202
2	100	168	236	336	404
3	150	252	354	504	606
4	200	336	470	672	808
5	250	420	588	840	1008

By combining the information from these two tables you can:

1. Nominate your room rate and thus set your daily guest room income, for our example £/€170.

2. Estimate your occupancy rates and thereby establish your anticipated yearly bed nights.

3. Combine both to estimate your potential income. In the following tables, we do just this.

Stand-alone commercial venture

Table 16 Potential guest room income

Guest room	15% £/€170	25% £/€170	35% £/€170	50% £/€170	60% £/€170
1	8,500	14,280	20,060	28,560	34,340
2	17,000	28,560	40,120	57,120	68,680
3	25,500	42,840	60,180	85,680	103,020
4	34,000	57,120	80,240	114,240	137,360
5	42,500	71,400	100,300	142,800	171,700

From Table 13, the stand-alone commercial venture in our exercise would require five guest rooms, at a room rate of £/€170 and an occupancy level of slightly more than 50% to achieve the £/€143,520 yearly sales target needed.

The industry average occupancy rate for a well-run B&B establishment located in an area where you can attract the corporate market mid-week and the leisure market during the weekends, ranges from 40% to 60%

Life-style adjustment

Table 17 Potential guest room income

Guest room	15% £/€140	25% £/€140	35% £/€140	50% £/€140	60% £/€140
1	7,056	11,760	16,520	23,520	28,280
2	14,000	23,520	33,040	47,040	56,560
3	21,000	35,280	49,560	70.560	84,840
4	28,000	47,040	66,080	94,080	113,120
5	35,000	58,800	82,320	117,600	141,400

The life-style adjustment in our exercise above would require a minimum of three guest rooms, a room rate of £/€140 and an occupancy level of slightly less than 26%. The average occupancy rate based on mostly weekend trade, ranges from 20% to 30%.

Playing 'What if?' and making a decision

Step 8. You have now reached the stage where you can compare your potential income with the income you need if you are to match or exceed your break-even point that we calculated in Step 6.

If your potential income is below your break-even level, we suggest that you go back to your earlier work, re-evaluate your cost options, expenditures, etc. and see the effect as you recalculate. You can ask the question: 'What would happen if?'

◆ you achieved cost savings in materials, guest amenities, etc.
◆ you modified your design
◆ you were able to raise your room rates
◆ you could increase your occupancy rate
◆ you discounted midweek room rates.

By asking these 'what if? type questions, you are, in effect, looking at possible modifications that could make your business idea more compatible with your personal needs and objectives.

YOUR DECISION

It is now the moment of truth! Your feasibility study is, as we stated earlier, simply a formalised approach to assist you in making your investment decisions. It provides you with a facility to evaluate your options every step of the way. It will not, however, make the final decision for you. You alone can make that decision.

TIP

Remember the old adage: you have to spend money to make money. Doing things on the cheap is usually a waste of your hard-earned savings.

If your decision was simply a matter of evaluating the economic viability of your proposed B&B, then such a decision would be an easy one to make. However, there are other key factors which impact on your final decision to proceed. These non-economic factors are:

◆ your private/family lifestyle expectations

◆ the willingness of your partner/family to match you in your commitment as a totally professional host

◆ your understanding of the difference between a life-style adjustment and a stand-alone commercial venture.

After looking at the results of the viability of your proposal and also at the non-economic factors we have just mentioned, you may decide **not** to proceed with your Bed & Breakfast proposal. If this is the situation, then the feasibility study you have just completed has still been a worthwhile exercise. It is a lot easier to withdraw at this stage than it is once your venture is actually up and running.

If, however, you conclude that your venture **is** viable and that you want to proceed, then the knowledge gained from your feasibility study is invaluable and will form the basis for your business plan when you write one.

We repeat our earlier advice to you to make full use of your professional team when you are writing this study. Finally, we wish you every success in your deliberations. Be reassured that you have taken the first step in a professional approach to getting into Bed & Breakfast.

This section includes extractions from the title *A Feasibility Study for Aspiring Bed & Breakfast Operators* by Stewart Whyte with Wal Reynolds.

The entire book can be purchased in a down-loadable, interactive format that enables you to create your own feasibility study. To obtain a download go to: www.bnb-central.com – click British Flag then Order Publications.

TIP

Keep yourself up to date with short-break holiday trends. This market segment has taken off.

Part Two

How to Run Your Bed & Breakfast Efficiently and Successfully

7

Putting the People Back in Service

S ervice. It is a word that you will hear over and over again in this chapter. Being willing and able to provide exceptional customer service is one of the keys to being a successful Bed & Breakfast operator.

We spoke in the first section of the book about whether you were the right sort of person to be a Bed & Breakfast host. By now we can assume that your positives outweighed your negatives. Get your answers to the questions from Chapter 1 and read them again. Are your answers the same?

There is no doubt that having had some prior experience in a service industry will stand you in good stead when running a Bed & Breakfast. But if you have not had the advantage of this experience all is not lost. You have been a consumer your whole adult life. Take some time to think about the best service that you have ever received when on holiday. What made it so good? What about the worst service? What was bad about it?

Service is a strange entity. If is often about perception. To one customer your behaviour may seem cloying and intrusive, to the next, receiving exactly the same service, you might seem remote and cold. The level of service is the same, but your guest has perceived it differently. Often the perception of good service isn't about how guests feel about you at all. Freshly ground coffee first thing in the morning, the morning paper outside their bedroom door, freshly baked scones for afternoon tea – these are things that can make up good 'service' in your guests' minds.

In this chapter we are going to focus on how you can ensure all the dealings you have with your guests are consistent and special for them.

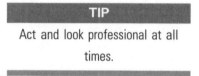

TIP

Act and look professional at all times.

COMMUNICATING WITH PROSPECTIVE GUESTS

My name is...

Your name is an integral part of making your guests feel at home. All of your interactions with your guests, whether on the telephone, by email, or in person should be personal and nothing will get this across as quickly as using your guest's name and they using yours. Introduce yourself by your first name and ask your guest if they would mind if you used theirs. People stay at B&Bs because they like the feeling of intimacy and 'home' that they represent. Using your first name, and theirs, is an easy way to give your guests an identity, and make them feel part of your family – if even for a day.

Telephone and fax

Ideally, you will want to invest in the installation of a separate line from that of your home phone. For a small price you can ensure that the call is for your business and you can answer accordingly. It also allows other members of the household to make personal calls without fear of missing a booking. It is suggested that if you have young children you prevent them from answering this phone. If you are going out you can either divert your **business phone** to your mobile (another necessity) or switch on your answering machine.

For those of you without a fax modem (shame on you!), a **fax** machine is an essential tool, given that you may wish to send your guest a sketch map showing how to find your B&B.

Answering the phone

Answer the phone with the name of your establishment and your name. Smile when speaking on the phone, it shines through and you can hear it. Always sound friendly, relaxed and courteous – you have already acknowledged you are a people person so this should be very easy.

You need your **reservation diary** and a **pen** by the telephone. You don't want to have to ask your caller to wait while you get organised – it doesn't leave a good impression. It is a great idea to ask questions of your caller so you can determine things that may be of interest of them and build some rapport with them as soon as possible. Note the kind of language a guest uses, so that you can match the style when you are talking to them later. By matching your caller's voice tone you will make them feel comfortable with you. They will also give you much more useful information if they feel you empathise with them.

Most of all you need to remember that much of your business will be won or lost by the information you present to your

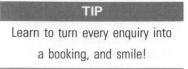

TIP

Learn to turn every enquiry into a booking, and smile!

customer over the telephone or email and how you present it.

Email

It is a very different world from even five years ago. Over the past five years the **Internet** has exploded and the reality is that much of the communication you have with potential guests will be over the Internet. Over 38% of Internet users have used it to book accommodation over the last 12 months. This is a statistic that is destined to grow over time.

For potential international and corporate guests, the Internet and email will be the main form of communication. It has the enormous advantage of being cheap and comprehensive, not to mention visual.

Ensure that the tone of your email is friendly yet professional. You need to check your emails regularly and follow up any inquiries promptly. Check your spelling and grammar, as even something as minor as this can deter some potential guests. They may believe that if you care so little for your business that you did not take the time to run a spell check you might not care about the details of their stay.

Questions

As much of your business will be won or lost by what you say over the phone, or in an email, there are a number of commonly asked questions that you should have the answer to.

The following is a list that you might like to start with. As people ask other questions write the answer down and put them with this list in the front of your reservation diary.

How can we reach you?

You need to be able to provide detailed directions on how your guest might reach you by car, public transport or walking, particularly if you are down unnamed lanes or a little out of the way. You might also give some idea of travelling time and distance. Ask the potential guest for their address, fax or email so you can send them a map. Directions should assume your guests are arriving with a tired, hungry family on a dark, wet night. Your directions should be so good that they are able to find you without any assistance. If you have specific parking instructions (for example, some local authorities will not allow on-street parking) you will need to be able to provide this information as well. They may even ask you to detail how close you are to local attractions with instructions on how they might get there. Check in and check out times are also important.

Once your guest confirms the booking you will need to pin point their arrival time as closely as possible, so you can ensure you are prepared.

RESERVATION DETAILS

You need to be able to present room rates and feature details as a friendly sales person would. This is your chance to win the guest's business. Now is your opportunity to advise: how far ahead you need booking confirmation, of your availability, of any minimum night restrictions (two nights at a weekend, for example), deposit details (how much, refundable or non-refundable) and cancellation penalties. At this initial stage, you will also need to advise how you accept payment – cash, cheque, credit cards, etc.

TIP

Offer to help plan a local itinerary. This can be done initially in your welcoming letter or upon your guests arrival.

So what do you need to record?

On arrival you need to ensure that you have the following guest information for your records: full name, address and nationality, plus – for all non-British/Irish or Commonwealth guests – their passport number, country of origin, arrival and departure times along with next destination point. (Diplomats do not need to register.) These records should be kept for a period of five years.

Ask your bank for the application forms that would ultimately enable you to process MasterCard, Visa and Bankcard. Many of your guests will expect this payment option; more details on this later.

FEATURES AND BENEFITS

You will often be asked by potential guests to provide the **features and benefits** of your establishment: the size of your rooms; any theme rooms you might have, e.g. decorated on a nationality theme; bed configuration; whether or not the room is serviced daily; whether the bathrooms are shared or if you have en suites; if you have a spa bath in any of the rooms. This is your opportunity to promote your Bed & Breakfast. You need to be able to talk about the meals you provide, whether they eat with you or privately, you may even be asked to provide some sample menus.

You may be asked about alcohol, whether it can be bought nearby, or if it is BYO (Bring Your Own). Some guests, especially from abroad, may ask whether there are cooking facilities they can use, a small kitchenette, or BBQ in summer. Any extras you provide such as laundry facilities, irons, hairdryers, phone lines, Internet access, etc., also need to be detailed here. If you have special packages for honeymoons, corporate clients, special school events or special interests, now is the time to offer to tell your potential guest about them.

CHILDREN, PETS AND SMOKING?

By now you will have determined your policy on these issues and you need to detail these to all prospective bookings.

> **TIP**
>
> Always tell your guest at the time of booking that there is a no-smoking policy.

Better your guests know your stance now rather than having a possible confrontation when they arrive.

SPECIAL NEEDS

Guests may ask you whether you have **facilities for the disabled** and you will need to be able to advise them about any modifications you have made. If you don't have appropriate facilities (such as wheelchair access) you need to tell them. **Dietary specialities** are another need you may be asked to cater for. If you provide an evening meal you may wish to ask at the point of reservation whether any of the party have any food restrictions, so you can plan in advance.

LOCAL ACTIVITIES AND ATTRACTIONS

You need to know *everything* about your local area, as guests will have the expectation that you are their local guide to the area.

Sell the best parts of your locality to your potential guests as this could sway them in your direction and also in the duration of their stay. You also need to be able to provide details of great places to eat in your area. Guests may ask you to send menus of

TIP

Be part of your guests' holiday by being available for general conversation and helpful advice.

local pubs and restaurants or even make bookings for them.

WRITTEN CORRESPONDENCE

A **letter** should follow up any telephone inquiries about your establishment, preferably the next day. This letter needs to be neatly presented and on a letterhead. As with email, correct spelling is paramount.

The letter should not give the impression of being a standard form, even if is. Try to personalise the letter with some information that your caller asked over the phone and use their first names, as well as yours.

If you are replying to particular questions, answer these questions specifically, not with 'our brochure is enclosed', although by all means enclose your brochure as well.

Once people have booked a room, follow up their booking with a written confirmation and a map. It is details like this that will make a difference.

DEPOSITS AND CANCELLATIONS

Normally, the booking arrangement must be honoured once the guest has accepted it. The only time it can be changed is when both parties agree. Larger properties and booking agencies tend to have lengthy deposit and cancellation policies whereas smaller operators need only to have a simple set of procedures.

The deposit taken at the time the booking is made ranges from 20 to 50% of the tariff, which maybe influenced by seasonal considerations.

The cancellation policy should be in writing and could reflect the following formula:

Days prior to booking commencement	As a percentage of total booking amount
0–12 days	100
13–21 days	75
22–42 days	60
43–60 days	33
93 days or more	10

When to claim

You can claim the amount owing after the duration of the booked stay has elapsed.

HERE AT LAST

Now is the moment you have been waiting for – the moment you come face to face with your guests and welcome them to your Bed & Breakfast. Again, you need to do your best to put your guests at ease immediately so they feel they are at their home away from home. Introduce yourself by your first name and if you know your guest's first name, use it with permission, as it will help put everyone at ease.

Ideally, when the guests arrive, and after they have freshened up, show them around and suggest that they come and join you for a quality drink and some freshly baked goodies.

The morning/afternoon tea has multiple purposes:

- it will allow you to get to know one another
- you can find out what they intend to do while staying in your area and it will allow you the opportunity to offer suggestions
- it will give you the opportunity to show off your baking skills.

The provision of a hot breakfast and freshly baked goods are cited as two of the main reasons people like to stay in Bed & Breakfasts.

When dealing with your guests there are a number of things you can use that will help you to achieve the perception of fantastic service.

BE ATTENTIVE

> **TIP**
>
> Guests want to be nurtured not smothered!

You need to appear interested in what your guests say. Remember the information they are giving you will help you make their stay special. You do, however, need to learn how to extricate yourself from a clinging guest without leaving them thinking you don't have time for them.

Your body language

Try to match **body language** in a subtle way. Face your guests directly. Don't fiddle or fidget – it gives the impression of boredom and nervousness. You want your guests to feel you are both comfortable and interested.

Maintain eye contact

The majority of people will believe you are uninterested in them if you do not have eye contact with them. They may also mistrust your sincerity.

Match your tone of voice to your meaning

You need to ensure that you sound like you mean what you say, and say what you mean. A mismatch will be evident to your listener. Try to modulate your voice and match the tone to your guest's.

Build rapport

From the first contact with your guest, take a few minutes to build rapport. This is easy to do with people you know or like, but it takes real professionalism to achieve it with people you don't know or like. You need to learn how to do it with conscious skill. The easiest way to do this is with body language. Be subtle here, matching the angle and position of the head and torso and only approximating the position of the arms and legs, it is these that will make your mirroring obvious if you imitate your guests too closely. Note the language your guests use and try to use similar words, matching the tone and speed of their voice. These may sound like very simple suggestions, but they have remarkably powerful effects.

Try them out first on people other than your guests, so that when you use these skills on your guests you can also pay attention to what they are saying until your rapport-building skills become automatic.

DRESS FOR SUCCESS

Your outward appearance is a personification of how your guests will view your establishment. If you dress well and look after yourself your guests will believe you take the same care of your establishment. You need to ensure you are always dressed in 'dressy casual'. For men, that might be a pair of slacks with a casual shirt. For women it is something you would be comfortable going to lunch in. Your hair should be clean and well groomed.

Your nails should be clean and well trimmed. For women, make up should be subtle. You need to ensure your breath is fresh and you have an absence of body odour.

If you are serving dinner we would suggest a change of clothes. You want to give your guests a bit of 'theatre'.

Always be aware of your attire. Primarily, it is the male partner we are concerned with here. Don't be caught out! The suitably attired female partner in the Bed & Breakfast venture may need to race down to the local shop to get something, and her partner, up to his eyes in gardening, says, 'If the guests arrive while you are out I will look after them'. A nice thought, but is this casual approach going to appear professional in the eyes of a paying guest?

When cleaning, wear clothes that are easy to launder, neat and do not show the dirt. Your shoes should have rubber soles in the interest of safety. Remove any jewellery when cooking or cleaning as it may be damaged by the cleaning agents and has a tendency to promote skin irritations.

SMOKING
No matter what your decision is regarding smoking, you personally should not smoke inside in front of guests. You should never smoke while working. Nothing is more offensive than one hand on a vacuum cleaner while the other is holding a lit cigarette. It is all about professionalism.

BEHAVIOUR
This is where your people skills come in. If your guests look like they want to be left alone, then respect their privacy. If, on the other hand, your guests want to chat, then remember it's in your time and subsequently you may need to determine the duration. This is a skill you will need to master.

You need to always work as quietly as possible. When guests come and stay with you, they are there to relax. They will often read, sleep in, or just rest. You want to minimise any negative impact you may have on them.

When it comes to conversation there are a few golden rules.

♦ Never talk about religion, sex or politics until it is safely established that these topics are acceptable. Don't be baited into getting into these topics with your guests. Such discussions usually end badly.

♦ Be friendly and nice, but don't over host: present an aura of friendliness that doesn't tip over into familiarity. Be available to your guests for helpful advice.

♦ After breakfast is a great time to offer some suggestions about things to see and do in your area.

♦ Never speak to your guests about your personal problems or concerns. Your guests have sometimes come away to have a break from their problems – never burden them with yours.

> **TIP**
> Recognise your guest's need for privacy.

STAFF

All the following information should be true of any staff you hire – from the casual who comes in once a fortnight to help clean, to a full-time chef, if you are the proprietor of a larger establishment.

Do not rush into **hiring staff**, for in the first few years of a non-established Bed & Breakfast you will gain considerable cost savings if you can do much of the work yourself. It is also much easier to manage staff if you have the experience of doing their type of work.

If you decide you need to hire labour you need to consider the following:

- Work out a job description with clear duties and expectations.

- Ensure that your employees understand exactly what is expected of them and that you will be performance managing them to those criteria.

- Obtain a copy of any union agreement or award from the appropriate union body.

- Develop a win-win agreement where performance will be monitored regularly and rewarded appropriately. If you need to performance manage you will then have an appropriate forum in which to do so. The ability to retain employees will serve you in good stead for the future.

- Ask your staff to bring **feedback** to their performance appraisals – from you or your partner, from a fellow staff member and from a guest or supplier.

- Train your staff regularly on different areas of your business. Everyone should have training on customer service and occupational health and safety.

Hold a weekly staff meeting for general news and information and for everyone to have their say. Use this forum to update your staff on your business goals and performance. This is also a great time to recognise and reward employees who are performing well.

ENTERING A GUEST BEDROOM

Even though it may be a room in your house, while guests are paying for accommodation, it is their room. There may be a time, however, during a guests' stay that you may need to enter their bedroom, to make their beds, etc.

To avoid any possible embarrassment to either party you should follow a few simple and easy rules.

Always knock on the door and wait for an answer. If after 20 seconds there is no reply knock again. If again there is no answer you should call out a greeting 'Good morning/afternoon' and enter the room. If you are there to clean the room and your guests are still there, ask them if they wish you to come back later. Don't ever knock on a room that has a 'Do not disturb' sign displayed. It is a good idea to provide these in all rooms for your guests' use – it helps you as a signal on whether or not they wish to be disturbed.

Some B&Bs advise their guests that the host's normal procedure is to stay out of their room unless the guest has a specific need that requires someone to go in there.

GUEST BEHAVIOUR

You have some liberties here if your Bed & Breakfast is also your home. You have the right to set rules such as how much alcohol can be consumed, noise levels, etc. How you monitor this, and to what length you wish to go is a more difficult question.

The main reason you may want to comment on a guest's behaviour is if it is disturbing you or other guests, if you suspect damage to your property, or if you suspect some illegal activity is occurring.

If you have to confront your guests about their **behaviour** you should do so in person, and in private. If the problem is occurring in the guest bedroom approach your guest there. Don't enter the room, but conduct your conversation at the door, and try not to sound judgemental. Instead, gently advise your guest of the nature of the complaint and the suggested appropriate behaviour. Thank them for their time and excuse yourself.

If the guest's behaviour does not improve you need to follow up your concern with the guest. Explain to the guest that it is your policy that the comfort of all of your guests is paramount, and that one individual guest cannot disturb the peace of others. Ask for the guest to show consideration to their fellow guests.

In most cases this will be enough, however in rare cases you may have to ask the guest to leave. If they refuse you will need to contact the police. If you have the unhappy experience of this happening you need to ensure that you are discreet in your handling of the affair, and keep the disturbance of any other guest to a minimum.

If on entering a room you find damage to your property you should make a report of it and add it to your guest's bill. If the guest has already checked out you should forward an account of the damage to the offender.

SEXUAL HARASSMENT

It rarely occurs in the Bed & Breakfast environment, but you may, at some time, be the victim of sexual harassment. **Sexual harassment** is an unwanted sexual advance, a request for sexual favours, or any unwelcome conduct of a sexual nature. Sexual harassment is not mutual attraction between two parties. Sexual harassment is against the law.

Under the Sex Discrimination Act, management has a duty to prevent sexual harassment and you, the employer, may be responsible if it occurs to one of your employees unless all reasonable steps have been taken to prevent it.

If you are being harassed you need to make your objections very clear to the harasser. Make a diary note about it. If the harasser tries to make fun of you or acts unaware, repeat clearly your objection and your wish that it will cease immediately. If it continues and the harasser is in your employ, that is sufficient reason for dismissal. You must contact the police if it is a criminal offence such as rape. That said, we have not heard of one case around the world where a staff member of a Bed & Breakfast has been the victim of any form of assault by a guest.

NEIGHBOURS

Your neighbours' feelings about your Bed & Breakfast venture are going to be a key to your success. They are going to be near you every day of the year, not just during the fleeting stays of your visitors.

They are not getting any financial benefit from your venture so you need to ensure that you minimise any impact on them. There are a few things you can do to make this relationship easier:

◆ Make sure that your guests are aware of any rights of way and do not block your neighbours' access, and make sure your guests know where your property ends and your neighbour's property begins.

- Try to ensure that you follow disturbance rules regarding noise.

- Take the time to get to know your neighbours.

- Take them one of the treats you make your guests occasionally, or invite them in for coffee. Little gestures like this will pay off.

COMPLAINTS

It is human nature. Occasionally you are going to have a customer who believes your best is not good enough. You need to use these complaints to your advantage; they are valuable feedback, which will enable you to refine your product. You will find that very few people will complain, but when you investigate you may find that other guests feel the same way. Every complaint will be different. You need to ensure that your establishment has a procedure for dealing with complaints, which everyone understands.

A correctly handled complaint can actually increase goodwill in your business. If you don't train your employees in dealing with complaints you could in effect serve to amplify the problem to a level that could substantially damage your business.

The following are some guidelines you should consider in your handling of complaints.

Don't underestimate the power of listening

Look your guest directly in the eye, face them and listen to what they have to say. It is often a good idea to offer your guest a seat. Sit down as well; you do not want to seem intimidating.

Do not take the complaint personally

Your guest will often be upset with a situation, not with you. Speak quietly. This works very well if your guest is raising their voice. Their volume will be unconsciously lowered to match yours.

Apologise

A statement like 'I am sorry you feel that way' does not admit fault but acknowledges your guest's feelings. Do not make excuses or trivialise the complaint. The customer only wants to know you are taking the grievance seriously. Avoid being drawn into a right and wrong argument. *Even if you win the argument, you will end up the loser if you make the guest feel trivialised.*

Deal with the complaint in a timely manner

If you need to investigate the matter further, ask your guest's permission to do so. While you are investigating offer your guest a cup of coffee.

If the complaint is about a meal, replace it. No questions asked. Bad food will leave a bad taste in your guest's mouth in more ways than one.

Keep control of the situation

The more unreasonable and irate your guest may be the more important it is that you stay cool, calm and collected. You need to look at the encounter as a challenge – *who can be the calmest, wins*. Adopt a constructive businesslike attitude. This will help move the sphere of the encounter from emotion to reason.

Never patronise or humiliate a guest

This can have disastrous results, and in the event that the mistake was yours or a member of your staff's, you will be the one who will be humiliated.

Follow up

Ensure that your guest was happy with your decision. Sometimes we believe we have settled a matter appropriately, only to find out, too late, that the guest was not at all happy. You must clarify the situation for mutual satisfaction.

The next step

Fixing complaints in the short term is one thing, fixing the long-term problem is just as important. In order to analyse complaints you need to put yourself in your guest's shoes and then ask yourself the following questions.

- Is the complaint justified? Is it a disagreement with your establishment's policy or with a matter of principle?

- Is the complaint genuine? Is it the result of a unique situation, a personality clash, or a genuinely difficult customer? (Trust us – they do exist.)

- Is it the first time you have heard the complaint, or is this complaint a frequent one?

- Is it a problem with a person or a system?

- Is it a trivial matter that has grown in size or intensity because of neglect?

After analysing the answers to the above you need to set up a process to prevent it from happening again. If the complaint was about a person other than yourself, you need to address the problem immediately. Use the same principles of listening and empathy that you used with your guest. Ensure, however, your staff member understands the importance of guest happiness in your business.

THE IMPORTANCE OF FEEDBACK

As we have said before, feedback, both positive and negative, can be the most important tool in the ongoing success of your business. Most guests won't express dissatisfaction directly to you, but would be most happy to fill in a **questionnaire.**

You can leave the questionnaire in the bedroom, accompanied by a thank you letter and a stamped, self-addressed envelope. Your guest is given the option of leaving the questionnaire or posting it, or sending it by email after their stay. This action will demonstrate you are interested in their considered comments.

As an incentive for filling in the questionnaire, you could offer your guests a bonus, such as 'Stay three nights, get one free', and advise them of cooking schools, fishing weekends, gourmet dinners, family fortnights, etc., that they may wish to take advantage of.

You can also advise them of events in your local community they might be interested in and any changes you may have made to your establishment (the addition of a spa bath in one of the bedrooms, for example).

> **TIP**
>
> You might consider a quarterly, one-page newsletter that points out forthcoming events in your area that, from knowledge gained from past guests, would be of interest.

Make sure your phone is manned as much as possible as most guests want to speak to the proprietor of a Bed & Breakfast, at some stage, before they book. How you conduct yourself during that conversation will often determine whether or not you clinch the booking. Don't let your personal worries intrude into your telephone manner. You must always sound as if you haven't a care in the world, and you're the warmest, most caring and hospitable person imaginable. That doesn't mean that you have to pour on the syrup with a ladle – insincerity will work against you as much as being grumpy. Just be pleasant, ready to please, and – be yourself.

If you have to set the answering machine, and most of us do at some time, *do* record a message that reflects your character. *Don't* leave some morbid tone that would be more appropriate for a funeral parlour! If you can, make it mildly humorous, or something that reflects the service you offer. If you're not confident you can record a good message – get someone who can.

Try to think of ways you can supplement your Bed & Breakfast income. If you have a historic house perhaps you can open it for public inspection. Garden open days are also very popular. If your garden is your pride and joy you may be able to take part in your community's open programme each a year. You can charge admission, which you can pour back into maintaining the garden. If you have a beautiful front parlour you may be able to hire it out to community groups for their monthly meetings.

You many need to be resourceful in the first few years to build both positive word of mouth acknowledgement and for your income generation.

GUEST QUESTIONNAIRE
HELEN'S Place

As part of our ongoing commitment for excellence, we ask that you fill in the spaces beside the questions and leave it here, or post it back to us using the reply paid envelope. It should be mentioned that the contents are for research purposes only and will remain confidential.

As a token of our appreciation, we will place your name in our annual lucky draw for a free, two-night stay in our Bed & Breakfast. The results of the draw will be mailed to you at the end of this year.

Name and address:..

Phone no:..

Was your stay with us up to your expectations? Y N (circle)

Please explain why: ....

Was Helen's Place easy to find? Y N

How do you believe we could improve Helen's Place?....................
....

What was the purpose of your visit in our area?..........................
....

Have you any plans to come our way again?..............................
....

Will you recommend Helen's Place to your friends? Y N

Would you be interested in receiving Helen's Place Gazette, our quarterly newsletter? Y N

Thank you, and please don't forget to leave this or post it in the envelope provided to:

PO BOX 0000,
Your Town. Post Code.

Helen and Warren Smith.

8

Housekeeping

I 've said it before and I will say it again. Housekeeping is the centrepiece of successful Bed & Breakfast operation. Any existing host will tell you that *if you are not fond of housekeeping, and if you are not particularly good at it, then Bed and Breakfast is not for you.*

TIP

Uphold a visible standard of cleanliness!

Look around your house. Are you one of those people where everything has a place? Do you regularly clean under the beds? Do you lift all your ornaments up and individually wipe them and the surface beneath them every time you clean? Do you clean around plugholes with a toothbrush? Does your house have the air of a magazine layout?

You do and it does? Good! You are exactly the sort of person who should run a Bed & Breakfast. You can never be too clean when operating a B&B. Cleanliness that is good enough for friends and family may not be good enough for paying guests. The two things that will destroy your reputation as a host are bad beds, and therefore a bad night's sleep, and a 'dirty' house.

Remember that your idea of a clean house may not be the same as your guests. Think of Felix Unger of *The Odd Couple*, he was the neat freak. Now multiply him tenfold. That is the standard you need to reach.

Even though your guest has chosen Bed & Breakfast for its 'homely' atmosphere, what they actually want is the picture book version of home. They want everything to be spotlessly clean and sparkling. They don't want to be reminded of the hundreds of guests who have stayed in the room before them. They want to feel that the room is as new. Immaculate cleanliness is the best way to achieve this and it will win you brownie points in the word of mouth stakes.

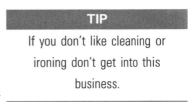

TIP

If you don't like cleaning or ironing don't get into this business.

BEING PREPARED

When getting ready to clean ensure that you are suitably attired. Wear flat, rubber soled shoes and gloves. Be very careful when emptying rubbish bins, as you do not know what people have left behind.

Having a cupboard in your laundry designated for cleaning products is a good idea. Make sure that you know what chemicals are in each product and the treatment in event of accidental poisoning.

A CLEANING CHECKLIST

We would suggest that you create a **checklist** for cleaning each room. This will serve as a reminder that you have covered everything when setting up for your guest, and as a guide for any outside help. The list below can be used as a guide, but you may

TIP

When cleaning watch for small details as the big things always get done.

need to add items based on your facilities.

Bathrooms

◆ Use disinfectant to clean the toilet bowl, inside and out.

◆ Mop the floor.

◆ Polish glass and mirrors.

◆ Scrub the bath and shower. If you have a spa bath or jacuzzi clean it thoroughly using recommended products. These can be a hotbed for germs, particularly jacuzzis, if you don't take special care.

◆ Unclog any drains.

◆ Empty rubbish bins.

◆ Disinfect all surfaces.

◆ Throw out any used soap, shampoo and conditioner.

◆ Wipe down any ornaments and decorative items.

◆ Wipe down all drawers, inside and out.

◆ Wipe down blinds and windowsills.

◆ Wipe shower curtains daily and machine wash them regularly to prevent mould.

◆ Remove any used towels, robes, etc.

◆ Restock toilet paper.

◆ Replace towels, hand towels and bath mats with clean ones, including spares.

◆ Replace robes with clean ones.

◆ Replace any toiletries you provide.

◆ Fill up the soap dispenser near the washbasin.

TIPS

Providing toiletries enhances the feeling of indulgence and can be a welcome relief to forgetful guests.
White towels absorb water better than coloured ones and can be bleached.

- Check that all the lights are working.
- Wipe down all the tiles.

Bedrooms
- Dust and polish all surfaces.
- Wipe down all ornaments.
- Polish glass and mirrors.
- Strip beds and replace sheets and pillowcases.
- Air blankets, pillows, blankets and continental quilts regularly.
- Sweep, vacuum and mop floors as appropriate, including under beds and furniture.
- Check that all light bulbs are working.
- Empty all rubbish bins.
- Put everything back in place.
- Check drawers for anything left behind. Anything left by guests should be isolated. Phone them and post it back.
- Wipe down windowsills and clean windows.
- Air the room by leaving windows open for at least an hour after every guest.
- Wipe down skirting boards and picture rails.
- Wipe down furniture.
- Check for any marks or scuffs on walls.
- Replace any used glasses or cups with clean ones.
- Replace any used coffee or tea.
- Replace any brochures, literature, discount coupons, etc.
- Use air freshener or light an aromatic candle.

TIPS
Provide two pillows and two towels per person. White linen is recommended as it does not fade, can be bleached and always matches. Guests should be able to read comfortably in bed. Have queen-sized beds rather than doubles as there are a lot of large and tall people around. Your sheets should be ironed slightly damp if they are 100% cotton.

Common rooms

- Dust and polish all surfaces.
- Wipe down all ornaments.
- Polish glass and mirrors.
- Sweep, vacuum and mop floors as appropriate, including under furniture.
- Vacuum under chair cushions.
- Wipe down furniture.
- Check all light bulbs are working.
- Empty all rubbish bins.
- Put everything back in place.
- Wipe down windowsills and clean windows.
- Wipe down skirting boards and picture rails.
- Check for any marks or scuffs on walls.
- Replace any brochures, literature, discount coupons, etc.
- Air the room as much as possible when there are no guests.
- Wipe down door handles.
- Wipe down telephone handsets.

TIP

Newspaper and water cleans glass quickly and effectively.

If you allow smoking in any of your common rooms ensure that you empty and rinse out ashtrays several times a day. Cigarette smoke is invasive and will become impregnated in all of your soft furnishing. We would also suggest always leaving a window open in this room to allow some of the smoke to escape.

Use air freshener or light an aromatic candle.

Kitchen

- Wipe down windowsills and clean windows.
- Wipe down skirting boards and picture rails.

◆ Check for any marks or scuffs on walls.

◆ Empty all rubbish bins at least daily.

◆ Sweep and mop floors at least daily or more frequently as required.

◆ Keep all surfaces clean from dust, food scraps and grease.

◆ Wash tea towels daily.

◆ Keep cloths clean and disinfected.

◆ Use the dishwasher where possible.

◆ Clean the oven regularly.

◆ Wipe down the fridge regularly.

◆ Wipe out cupboards and pantry weekly.

◆ Check that all light and power points are functioning.

> **TIP**
>
> Cloths: Use different colours for different purposes, one for the floor, one for washing up, one for wiping vegetable chopping boards, one for wiping meat chopping boards, etc.

> **TIP**
>
> Don't forget a fire extinguisher and a fire blanket in the kitchen.

TAKING CARE OF YOUR FURNITURE

You need to remember that your furniture has now also become the property of your guests. They, however, may not take as good care of it as you would. Thus, it becomes your responsibility to take care of it enough for all of you. Following are some hints to help you do this.

◆ Take care to handle your furniture carefully. Bumps will mar wooden furniture. When you need to vacuum or mop the floors, it is better to move the furniture.

◆ Any spills should be wiped immediately.

◆ Provide plenty of coasters on coffee tables, bedside tables, lamp tables, etc. and encourage guests to use them.

◆ Wipe furniture daily.

◆ Have your couches professionally cleaned regularly.

- A good cleaning fluid does wonders on most surfaces, including granite.
- Put adhesive felt on the bottom of ornaments to protect the surface of your furniture.

THE OUTSIDE

While cleaning the inside is important, ensure you don't forget the outside of your house. Any marks on your house façade should be fixed before they are a problem.

- Sweep paths to the house daily.
- Wipe down the outside of the door.
- Polish the letterbox, door handle, knocker and bell.
- Sweep and mop the entrance areas.
- Keep windows clean.
- Wipe down all of the outdoor furniture daily, so guests feel they can use it.
- Wipe down any tables after use.
- Mow lawns regularly.
- Keep paths free from weeds and overgrown plants and remove and replace plants as need dictates. Gardens need to be tended and your guests will appreciate the care you take of their sanctuary (and yours).

- Check outdoor lighting nightly to ensure the bulbs are functioning.
- Check roof tiles regularly. A loose tile can cause havoc inside and out.

9

Occupational Health and Safety

I t is your duty to yourself, your family, your employees and your guests to provide a safe place in which to live, work and stay. To help facilitate this we suggest you set down a few guidelines that will cover fire safety, work practices and general instructions for guests.

FIRE SAFETY
The first step is to contact your local fire authority and ask them to carry out a fire risk assessment.

Most B&Bs do not come under the Fire Precautions Act 1971 which require properties who accommodate more than six people (guests **or** staff), or if they have any sleeping accommodation above the first floor or below ground floor level to have a fire certificate. But this could change given the new legislation due out in October 2006.

Follow your local fire authority instructions to the letter and have them train you, your family and your staff on the use of the smother blanket and fire extinguisher which you are required to provide in the kitchen and common areas. Recommendations will involve such procedures as smoke alarms in every guest bedroom, in your own bedrooms, outside your kitchen and in hallways. Having a heritage listed home may give you a bit of leeway in the placement of alarms. You cannot legally, or morally for that matter, operate a Bed & Breakfast without smoke alarms.

Go round your house and replace any double adaptors with power boards. Double adaptors can be a main cause of domestic fires. Your insurance agent may also have certain requirements as part of your policy. Ensure that you adhere to any requirement that may be needed.

As guests check in draw their attention to your exits, the storage places for the smother blankets and fire extinguishers. Advise your guests of a common meeting place outside the property in the event of a fire.

Leave your reservation diary near the door at night so you can easily check everyone off and ensure all are safe.

Never deadlock your door while you or guests are inside. In the case of a fire you may not be able to escape.

A SAFE PLACE TO STAY

Room by room you need to establish that your house is as safe as it can possibly be.

In the **bathrooms** you need to ensure bathmats have non-slip backing, that the room is thoroughly disinfected after each guest's visit, that guests do not share bar soap and that no medication is kept in the bathroom. You might want to consider handrails near the bath and the shower.

The **kitchen** can be a hotbed for germs. You need to keep pets out of the kitchen and any dining areas. Any detergents and cleaning agents should be kept in a cupboard separate from food. Ensure you know how to treat poisoning that can occur from oral or eye contact with any of these agents. You should neither smoke nor eat when preparing food. Use separate cutting boards for meat and vegetables – label them accordingly. Keep fridge temperatures at 5° Celsius. Cover any wounds with band-aids and gloves. Ensure you reheat foods thoroughly. Cover food prior to serving. Wear gloves when preparing food as much as practicable. These aspects will be covered in your certificate of compliance. More detailed advice on safety in the kitchen is given later in this chapter.

In common areas you should ensure lighting is adequate, smoke detectors are in all guest bedrooms, hallways and common areas. Ensure that all stairs have handrails. Electrical wiring should be inspected regularly. Think about installing safety switches to protect you from power surges. Make sure rugs are taped down or have a non-slip backing. If you are planning on accommodating families, particularly toddlers, you might want to consider safety plugs for power points, safety latches on low cabinets and gates for stairs. Leave emergency numbers by the phone.

Outside you should ensure your property is well lit, that paving is in good repair and that any steps are not slippery.

A SAFE PLACE TO WORK

Not only should your Bed & Breakfast be a safe place to stay, you need to ensure it is a safe place to work.

Train your staff and your family on fire procedures and how to use extinguishers and smother blankets. Have quarterly evacuations to ensure everyone knows where the outside meeting point is.

Another safety precaution would be Hepatitis B vaccinations. Hepatitis is a rapidly spreading disease in all its permutations. As you are handling both food and cleaning it might be a good precaution to have this done. See your local doctor.

Wear clean clothes and rubber-based shoes when cleaning, as you don't want to spread germs. The most important thing you can wear when you clean, however, is a pair of gloves. It will protect you from all of the bacteria that you will encounter. Use different gloves for cleaning bathrooms than you would for cleaning any other room in the house. Do not touch your face with these gloves.

SAFETY IN THE KITCHEN

Safety in the kitchen is two-fold. It is about protecting you from accidents, in the most accident-prone place in your house, and protecting you and your guests from diseases, the obvious one being food poisoning.

In certain areas, you must undertake **food-handling courses** at your nearest accredited learning facility. If it is not compulsory in your area, we would recommend you consider one of the recognised courses. They are normally only one or two days and can save you and your business a lot of anguish in the long run. They will teach you about effective hygiene practices, food storage, cleaning and sanitising, avoiding food contamination, food legislation and understanding legal obligations.

The Food Safety Act 1990 applies to all businesses serving foods and in combination with Food Standards Agency (FSA) guidelines, sets minimum hygiene standards with particular reference to washing facilities, utensils, storage times and temperatures. You must inform your local authority environmental health officer 28 days before opening for business.

There are a number of things you can do that will minimise accidents in your kitchen.

- ◆ Don't rush around the kitchen. Working methodically is more productive in the long run and minimises any chance of slipping.

- ◆ Keep knives sharp and clean. Never wash them in soapy water with other items – someone is likely to cut him or herself. When sharpening knives do it away from your body. When wiping them do so with the sharp end pointed away from you. Always use the correct knife for the job.

- ◆ Your clothing should offer protection. Long sleeves will protect your arms from steam, and aprons will protect your body and clothes from the stove.

- ◆ Use a dry cloth or oven mitt when handling hot dinner plates and saucepans. A damp cloth will heat up, create steam, and ultimately result in a scald.

- Saucepan handles should not protrude over the edge of the stove as this can create accidents. Use two hands, protected with mitts, to carry saucepans.

- Arrange the oven shelves before you turn the oven on. This will help stop burns.

- Mop any spills immediately to prevent slipping.

THE FUTURE

While absolute food safety cannot be guaranteed by regulations, it is possible to minimise the risk to public health by introducing measures leading to improvements in hygienic production and handling of food, in direct response to the hazard posed. Contact your local health authority for requirements.

It is important to appreciate the significant costs attributable to food-borne disease (entire loss of business) and the savings that could be achieved as a result of the reform of food hygiene regulations. By reducing the incidence of food-borne illness, the proposed, risk-based, preventative food hygiene standards will have specific benefits for many sectors of the community including:

- If you provide evening meals and want to serve alcoholic drinks you'll need a licence. Get in touch with the Clerk to the Justices at your nearest magistrates court for more information.

- Even if all you plan to serve is a home-cooked breakfast you should inform your local environmental health department who may wish to inspect the premises on a regular basis (under the terms of the Food Safety Act 1990).

♦ **Consumers**: through fewer incidents of food-borne illness and lower associated medical costs.

♦ **The domestic food industry**: through increased consumer confidence and a move to less prescriptive and nationally uniform outcome based regulations.

♦ **Employers**, in both the private and public sectors: as less sick-leave would be taken due to the reduced influence of food-borne illness.

♦ **Other industry sectors**: such as tourism, which will benefit through increased customer confidence.

Identify the hazards: Some hazards can be controlled, while others may be beyond our control. For example, the quality of raw materials you receive is the responsibility of your suppliers.

Identify the critical control points: These are the points at which important processes can go wrong.

TIP
Wash all fruit and vegetables to remove soil, bacteria, insects and chemicals.

The difference between a critical control point (CCP) and a hazard is that a CCP can be controlled and monitored. Temperature control in chillers and cold-rooms is a good example of a CCP.

Set the critical limits for each CCP
If you exceed these limits you could face a major problem: for example if your cold-room were running at a temperature of 10°C, this would be a problem.

Monitor the CCPs: Every CCP will require monitoring to make sure you do not exceed the critical limit.

With the cold-room you would need to monitor the temperature using a hand-held thermometer.

Establish corrective action: Decide what action is to be taken if the critical limits are exceeded. If your cold-room is running too warm you should adjust the temperature or call the technician.

Set up records

This is one of the most important steps because records can prove your compliance. Records are also useful in training your staff and tracking results, for example, regularly recording the cold-room temperature on a chart.

Will my business have to comply?

Businesses, which provide, produce, or package food for consumption by the general public are required to comply with all existing legislation.

FIRST AID

We believe you have a moral, if not legal, obligation to be able to provide **first aid** to your staff and guests. One member of your staff or family being certified is probably enough, but it should be the person who is primarily running the establishment. Everyone in the household should know and understand your establishment's procedures for handling an emergency.

One thing you must do is purchase a comprehensive first aid kit. You need to maintain the kit and log any incidents that occur. Again, you can purchase this on the Internet through St John's Ambulance at www.sja.org.uk/

10

Food and the Bed & Breakfast

A ll Bed & Breakfasts and guest houses are requested by the Food Safety Act 1990 to register with the environmental health department that is attached to the local authority.

This is a requirement as set down by the Food Standards Agency, which has only recently been established. The registration is free of charge and the supplied form is easy to fill in.

In essence, the Agency requires you to keep food handling premises clean and that all food operations are carried out in an hygienic way.

We suggest strongly that you obtain a copy of the new regulation from either your local authority or by downloading it from the Internet.

We now reach the breakfast part of the Bed & Breakfast. Your house is ready, your marketing and business plans are in place, and your guests are on their way. What are you going to do about breakfast?

BREAKFAST OPTIONS

The fully cooked breakfast

This is your opportunity to shine. By now your guests should have had a glimmer of your cooking with afternoon tea on the day of their arrival. However, breakfast is the meal your guests have been waiting for. Most guests will be looking forward to the Great British, Scottish, Welsh, Ulster or Irish fry-up, that is, the famous **cooked breakfast** that is still so popular with many people on holiday.

Start with the basics: a few cereals, fresh fruit juice, fruit compote or fruit, freshly baked bread, conserves, speciality teas and brewed coffee. Muffins and croissants are a nice extra.

Your guests may not want all the above, but it should be on offer. What most will want is a hot meal and something different from what they would prepare at home. Our suggestion is that you offer a few different options for the guest to choose from.

The trick here is to be imaginative. Look in the hundreds of wonderful cookbooks that are released each year and experiment with them. Don't, however, experiment with your guests. If you want to try something new, try it on your friends and family first.

There are great recipes that have a twist on the traditional. For example, Eggs Benedict served on muffins with smoked salmon, French toast mixed with cinnamon sugar, and savoury pancakes and crêpes. You can run the gamut from the traditional to the experimental, but you should have fun with it.

You don't need to offer a huge variety every day. It is best is to have one or two special dishes available every day and to rotate them, so that guests who are staying more than one night have some variety. Having staples such as bacon, eggs, mushrooms and tomatoes in your cupboard will serve you well for those guests who prefer the more traditional fare.

As for quantity you don't want to scrimp. Most guests won't be greedy, but they will want a hearty breakfast. The one disadvantage of having breakfast in your type of accommodation is that some guests will feel they should be able to eat as much as possible. You will need to factor this into your room rate/tariff.

Presentation is almost as important as the food itself. When serving your breakfast you need to look at the aesthetic appearance of the food through the eyes of a paying guest. Take into account colour, texture and smell. The appreciation of food is through all five senses so you should ensure you consider all of them when serving your meal.

The continental breakfast

The **continental breakfast** traditionally consists of a croissant or Danish pastry with coffee or tea, and if you are lucky a glass of juice. Some Bed & Breakfasts are offering 'continental breakfast', but are actually providing fruit, toast, tea and coffee. We do not believe either of these options is good enough if you want to gain recognition as a superior Bed & Breakfast. Most guests use the occasion of staying in a Bed & Breakfast as an opportunity to experience a cooked breakfast – if they wanted tea and toast they would have stayed at home. However, the option of a simple breakfast with toast or a continental breakfast could be offered for those who desire a lighter meal.

The breakfast basket

The provision of a **breakfast basket** is popular with those guests who want to be out and about early, for example, walkers and cyclists. It can contain fresh juice, fresh fruit compotes with yoghurt, freshly baked bread with jams and conserves, butter, a thermos of tea or coffee and often freshly baked goods such as Danish pastries and muffins and the appropriate eating and drinking utensils. If there are cooking facilities you can also supply bacon, eggs, or freshly made speciality sausages.

> **TIP**
> Make your breakfasts exciting, if guests stay for more than one night vary the menu so they have a selling point for you, when talking to others.

Presentation is very important here. You won't have the opportunity to impress with your cooking, although the freshly baked goods will help, so you need to focus on how you are going to present your breakfast. Make your basket look like a gift to the guest. Linen serviettes, rolled in a decorative napkin ring, will add a special touch. Have a look in some cookbooks for ideas.

LUNCH

This is really up to you, and very few guests will expect it. If you do offer it, do so at an extra cost. Remember that preparing **lunch** for your guests will really break into your day. The amount you charge will never make up for the time you will have to spend preparing it.

A **picnic basket**, provided at an extra cost, is a popular option for the guests. This, as with the breakfast basket, is particularly popular in areas where people are likely to explore the natural wonders in the surrounding area. Preparation time is much the same as for an in-house lunch, but there is little cleaning up afterwards.

MORNING AND AFTERNOON TEA

As we have mentioned before it is a great idea to welcome your travel weary guests with **morning or afternoon** tea. The traditional version of this is tea or coffee with home-baked goodies, such as scones or pikelets.

Some B&Bs are experimenting here as well. They are welcoming their guests with cheese, dips and antipasto. The only drawback with this is it doesn't fill your house with the same aroma as freshly baked biscuits.

This is a great opportunity to catch up with your guests, find out their plans and give them some advice on your locality. You can use the opportunity to set down any house rules you might have and acquaint them with your fire escapes, etc.

If you have a large establishment you could provide a high tea, with dainty sandwiches and cakes, scones, a selection of wonderful teas and coffees and even the occasional string quartet. In this way you could add some theatre to your establishment and earn some extra money, making it an open house.

> **TIP**
> Always be prepared to make another pot of coffee and have refreshments freely available.

DINNER

Some Bed & Breakfasts and guest houses do a **weekend gourmet package**, which includes an evening meal for one or more nights. This is particularly useful if you don't have a variety of restaurants in your locality that you can happily recommend. Again, experiment with some of the wonderful cookbooks on the market and try to use as much local produce as possible. Any cookbook by local writers and cooks is a great place to start.

If your guest asks to stay in for dinner without much warning you need to do two things. Charge them, and let them know that they have to have what you happen to keep in stock, or they can have what you and your family are eating. The cost charged should reflect the meal you are serving.

If you are going to cook dinner be sure you purchase fresh meat from a quality butcher, fresh vegetables and fruit from a quality grocer and seafood from a specialist. Don't purchase these items from a supermarket, as the quality is not consistent. You want to be remembered as the host who provided a quality meal.

EATING WITH GUESTS

We don't suggest that you do because this is really up to you and your guests. It is quite a difficult meal to serve and eat at the same time. You will also find your guests will sleep in and you will need your strength for the day ahead. Of all international guests, Australians tend to be a bit shy at breakfast so let them have this meal to themselves.

I have found that many guests are frequently not very comfortable sharing breakfast tables with each other, tending to be a bit monosyllabic and uncommunicative. You might find it better to ensure you have a few separate tables where couples can have breakfast 'alone'. Ask them for their seating preference the evening before.

If you are serving dinner there is no reason why you should not eat with your guests. It is quite likely that if your guests have chosen to eat at home they would like some company. Don't overpower the conversation, but feel free to let your natural personality shine.

KNOWING THE RESTAURANTS, CAFES AND PUBS IN YOUR AREA

You need to become an expert on the cafes, restaurants and pubs in your area. This is one of the most important recommendations you will be asked to give. You need to have tried the restaurants you recommend as, like it or not, you will be judged on the quality of your recommendation.

By being part of your local tourism body you will meet many of the restaurateurs in your area. You may be able to arrange a 10% discount for your guests, or a free cup of coffee, or even a free meal for you and your partner for every ten recommendations you send their way. Never enter into an arrangement such as this, however, unless you really believe the restaurant is up to scratch. A 'free' dinner for you is no reason to destroy your credibility. Your reputation is worth much more than that.

PRESENTATION

It is very important that you present your food to the best of your ability. Whilst I am passionate about increasing the professionalism of the industry I am equally passionate about Bed & Breakfasts retaining their individuality, or what makes them unique. If it is your style to provide sugar in a sugar bowl, then, as long as you provide a sugar spoon, feel free to do so in your B&B. The same applies to jams and conserves. This is your home and it is these small touches that your guests will be looking forward to during their stay.

LIQUOR LICENCES

The Licensing Act 2003 as it applies to England, Wales and Scotland integrates various legislation and licensing systems that previously existed and consolidates these activities into a single Act.

The Act transfers the liquor licensing function from the magistrates court to the local authority and incorporates it with entertainment licensing legislation, the provision of late-night refreshment, cinemas, theatres and other licences under the newly created Licensing Authority.

The Act applies to any B&B or guest house operator where the owner intends to sell or supply alcohol or provide regulated entertainment or provide late night refreshment must have a premises licence. The premises licence holder must name a personal licence holder if the application includes the sale of alcohol.

This in effect means that you would need a liquor licence if you were to offer your guests a complimentary glass of alcohol, for the licensing authority would assume that you factored into your room rate the cost of the alcohol.

We asked Kenneth Morgan, at William Fry Solicitors, Dublin, a leading legal firm for their comments on the Liquor Licensing Act as it applies to Bed & Breakfast and guest house owners.

They gave us the following advice on the type of liquor licence available for Bed & Breakfast and guest house operators in the Republic of Ireland:

> The position in Ireland is governed by an Intoxicating Liquor Licensing code, which has application to all premises where alcohol is sold for consumption on or off the premises. A Licence is required in all circumstances for the retail sale of alcohol. The running of a Bed & Breakfast or a guest house is

governed by standards enforced by Bord Fáilte and the body known as Excellence in Tourism.

Where a B&B or guest house wishes to sell wine, an application for a Wine Retailer's On-Licence must be made to the Collector of Customs & Excise. An application to Court is not required. The Collector will authorise an official to visit the premises to verify that the premises are suitable for a Wine Retailer's On-Licence. The process will take one month; upon the expiry of that period and in the absence of any objections the Licence will issue upon payment of the Excise Duty. In our experience the issue of such licences is relatively straightforward. The Licence remains in force until the end of the licensing year – 30 September – and then must be renewed for the subsequent twelve months.

Where the Wine Retailer's On-Licence attaches to a 'restaurant', beer may be sold for consumption on the premises provided that the beer is consumed at the same time with a meal and paid for at the same time as the meal is paid for; the restaurant is not entitled to a bar counter.

To qualify as a restaurant, one must hold a Restaurant Certificate. This can only be obtained from the local District Court and must receive the consent of the Garda Síochána. The local Superintendent, in whose area the premises are located, must be satisfied that the application is *bona fide* and he/she will be represented at the court hearing.

It is important to emphasise that a B&B or guest house is not entitled to sell beer unless it attaches to a certified restaurant. Under no circumstances may spirits be sold on the premises unless the B&B or guest house has been granted a Special Restaurant Licence or a full Publican's Licence.

Whilst it may be the practice that a glass of wine or bottle of beer is provided as part of a meal on an informal basis in a B&B or guest house this amounts to a breach of the Licensing Code – unless offered gratuitously.

PURCHASING TIPS

The quality of your produce will be reflected in your meal. Your guests will expect as much **fresh produce**, preferably locally grown, as possible. One of the most important things you can do before even thinking of serving up a meal for your guests is to find suppliers for all of your food needs. Good suppliers for meat, fruit and vegetables, seafood and poultry are very important – as said before, you will rarely find the quality you need at a supermarket.

A good baker is handy, but with the proliferation of bread makers on the market there is no reason that you can't bake your own. Be aware when purchasing a bread maker that many suppress the aroma. Be wary of purchasing one of these – you want the smell of freshly baked bread wafting through the house. Your guests will love it.

A delicatessen is another worthwhile find. You will be able to purchase some fantastic cheeses here, and many other great treats.

RECIPE IDEAS

Nectarines in passionfruit syrup
$1/3$ cup sugar
½ cup passionfruit pulp (fresh or tinned)
2½ cups water
8 white nectarines, halved and stones removed

Place sugar, passionfruit and water into a deep, heavy base saucepan over a medium heat, simmer for five minutes until slightly syrupy. Add more sugar, if necessary. Add nectarines and simmer for one minute on both sides or until just soft.

Place nectarines in serving bowls, strain pips from passionfruit syrup, pour over nectarines. Serve warm or chilled.

Serves 4.

Baked peach brioche
8 small slices of brioche or fruit bread
100g cream cheese
3 tblsp castor sugar
1 tsp vanilla extract
4 peaches, sliced
$^1/_3$ cup of icing sugar

Place the brioche slices in a baking dish lined with baking paper or foil. Combine the cream cheese, sugar and vanilla in a bowl and spread on the brioche. Top with peach slices and sprinkle heavily with icing sugar. Bake in a preheated oven at 200°C for 20 minutes or until the peaches are golden. Serve warm or cold.

Raspberry puffs
1 cup self-raising flour
½ cup icing sugar
1 tsp baking power
2 eggs
60g butter, melted
½ cup milk
300g raspberries
Icing sugar and lemon wedges to serve

Place flour, icing sugar and baking powder in a bowl. Add eggs, butter and mix until smooth. Mix in raspberries.

Drop spoonfuls of mixture into a non-stick frying pan over a medium heat and cook until the puffs are golden.

To serve, sprinkle with icing sugar and a slice of lemon.

Serves 4.

Salmon puffs
Smoked salmon
2 leeks, cleaned and cut into rings, white part only

Filling
300g ricotta
300g Gruyère, grated
2 tblsps dill, chopped
2 tblsps capers, chopped

Mix filling together.

Filo pastry, 8 sheets
Brush every second sheet with soft butter.
Poppy seeds

Layer in an ovenproof dish or in individual muffin tins:

Two sheets pastry, filling, leeks, one or two rings for the individual puffs, salmon.

Top with two layers of pastry, brush with butter and sprinkle with poppy seeds.

Bake 200°C, 40 minutes for the large pie, 20 minutes for the individual pies.

Serves 6.

Mediterranean omelette
1 red capsicum
6 slices prosciutto, roughly chopped
3 spring onions thinly sliced
40g feta, crumbled
40g parmesan, grated
4 free range eggs
150ml milk
1 tsp olive oil

Cut capsicum into small flat pieces, place under a hot grill until skin blackens and blisters. Place in bowl. Cover tightly with plastic wrap, leave for ten minutes then rub off skin and discard. Cut capsicum into thin strips.

Heat olive oil in frying pan and sauté prosciutto until crisp. Whisk eggs and milk together, pour into oiled, ovenproof pan. Scatter capsicum, prosciutto and onions over eggs.

Bake 180°C, for 30 minutes or until filling is just set.

Serves 4–6.

Easy breakfast puff pie
½ cup chopped onion
½ cup chopped zucchini
2 oz cooked ham steak cubed
1 ¼ oz shredded cheddar cheese
2 tblsps sour cream
2 eggs (or 3 egg whites)
pinch pepper

Preheat oven to 350° Fahrenheit. Spray 9-inch pie plate with non-stick spray. Spray frying pan with non-stick spray; add onion, zucchini and ham. Cook for about two minutes until translucent. Spread union mixture over bottom of pie plate, add beaten eggs.

Sprinkle cheese on top. Bake until golden brown and puffy (35 to 45 minutes).

Serves 4.

Be as flexible as possible when it comes to **breakfast serving times**. Some guests like to take the opportunity to get up early, while others like to sleep in. There is no harm, however, in asking an approximate time the evening before so you can plan your day, or in letting your guest know when you plan to finish serving breakfast.

> **TIP**
>
> To check if an egg is fresh drop it gently in a glass of cold water. If it sinks it is fresh, but if it bounces up, it is not and it should not be used.

Like everything you do in this most competitive of businesses, your breakfasts must be first class. If you serve ordinary white bread, jams in sachets, longlife milk and a variety of cereals in little cardboard packets, you can be sure that if your guests do come back it won't be for the breakfasts!

Even if you consider yourself the world's worst cook, with a little help and imagination you can still come up with a great breakfast. With breadmaking machines and good quality flours available there's no excuse for serving the bland packaged breads that abound. You may have access to a really good bakery. If you do not, have a go at baking yourself. It's not hard and your guests will appreciate the effort. The same goes for jams and marmalades. If you don't fancy trying to make your own, there's nearly always a little old lady nearby who makes wonderful preserves. A little research and effort on your part will pay dividends. And remember, there's nothing wrong with bacon and eggs. Even if it isn't new and trendy, it's for good reason that it's the singular most endurable breakfast dish in the world! Just make sure the eggs are good and fresh and the bacon is top quality.

These days there are any number of specialists who make wonderful sausages and who will ensure delivery almost anywhere.

A recent survey indicated 95% of people enjoyed a cooked breakfast but 94% rarely ate one. However when people go on holiday they like to start the day with a cooked breakfast, so be prepared to oblige.

> **TIP**
>
> If all else fails, start baking. It fills the house with lovely aromas.

11

Day-to-Day Operations

S o your guests are here. You have your people skills off pat. You have established a business model that works for you. What you now need to do is look at the best way to run your business from day to day. You need to establish systems that will allow you to enjoy your new lifestyle, and provide your guests with a fantastic holiday experience.

BOOKINGS

We talked in an earlier chapter about the things you will need to communicate to prospective guests over the phone and the Internet. What we need to now talk about are the **bookings** themselves, primarily how you are going to record them.

For those of you starting your own Bed & Breakfast we would suggest you start with a **diary**. Divide each day into the number of rooms you have available. As you take bookings you should record the following information in the appropriate room:

- the date you took the booking
- the arrival and departure date of your guest
- the guest's name, address and phone number
- deposit information
- any comments, such as particular dietary requirements, estimated time of arrival, etc.

We would also suggest you set up a **reservation chart** at the front of the diary, or on the wall of your office, near your phone. This will help you see at a glance if you have rooms free on a requested date.

With both the chart and the diary it is a good idea to make your reservations in pencil, in case alterations are needed. Don't forget to block out days that you will not be taking guests on the chart and in the diary. For later reference place the reason next to these 'time off' days, for example holidays, family time, repairs, maintenance, etc. Any chance bookings, that is, guests who arrive without a reservation, should also be added to both the chart and the diary.

The other part of the booking is the **deposit.** We would suggest you take at least 25% as a deposit. Many Bed & Breakfasts are making these deposits non-refundable. You must specify this at the time of booking. For holidays and other busy times we suggest you take a larger deposit. Another good idea is to have minimum stays for events and long weekends, for example minimum three nights stay. This will ensure your occupancy is high and you don't miss out on other bookings during peak periods.

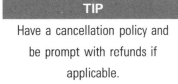

TIP

Have a cancellation policy and be prompt with refunds if applicable.

BOOKINGS AND THE INTERNET

We have talked above about the most basic way to record your bookings. However, in this new technical age, with many travellers utilising the **Internet** for bookings, we wanted to know what Bed & Breakfasts could do in this regard. We asked Gideon and Sara Stanley of Grace Software Inc, a recognised leader in reservation system design for Bed & Breakfasts, the following questions.

Question: Why does a B&B operator need to have a reservation system?

Answer: The property owner can manage their reservations, monitor marketing efforts and also make rooms available on the Internet for booking. For this you need an end-to-end reservation system.

With improvements in high-speed Internet access, software is now available in two platforms. The first is the traditional desktop software installed on the property's own PC, and the second is a web-based application which works through an Internet browser. Given that the data is stored in a secure server, means people can manage their reservations or make bookings from anywhere in the world, where you have Internet access. Regardless of the platform you select, the reservation software is the centre for all reservation, guest data, marketing and reporting activities.

Question: What is web-based property management software?

Answer: A web-based property management software integrates *all* reservations in one central database – which is located on a server computer *off* property. Consider this an 'ASP' model, which stands for application service provider. Instead of purchasing software upfront, the property owner would pay a monthly fee to use property management software hosted by the vendor on a remote secure server. The entire property management system would be accessed through a web browser interface.

CUSTOMER RELATIONSHIP MANAGEMENT

Some small property owners who have not yet bought into reservation software mistakenly think it's a matter of transferring paper reservation information to a computer system. An effective reservation system offers much more, including occupancy and income reports, the ability to monitor your marketing efforts and to store important details about your guests, which is readily available any time they return for a visit.

ONLINE RESERVATIONS

In recent years, the Internet has contributed to the marketing potential of a fully computerised reservation system. It has provided small and medium-sized properties with the same opportunity and power as the larger properties. Now small property managers can regulate their online reservations with the sophistication of the large hotel chains.

Question: Why is accessible accommodation availability important to a global reservation switch?

Answer: B&Bs and guest houses don't have enough business guests to justify a designated terminal and the costly links to global airline reservation systems like Sabre or Apollo. With individual accommodation providers having access to a global reservation facility plus booking engine, guests searching for places to stay on the Internet have access to both your reservation and property information. Providing immediate information about availability is critical for a small property. Often the first question a potential guest will ask concerns dates and availability. By offering this information on a web site, the guest's first concern is handled instantly and they can proceed by filling out a reservation form.

Because of the Internet, your property can now provide this immediate availability information, traditionally available only through the costly Sabre systems.

Question: What are the other advantages of having such an integrated system?

Answer: Marketing information at your fingertips.

As new guests arrive at your property, you can record their referral source and preferences. At a later date, this information can easily be compiled into a report that indicates which marketing venues are most effective, and perhaps how they are effective, e.g. certain packages or rooms.

What are your guests' preferences? For what kind of occasion do they visit your property? Knowing the answers to these questions better positions you to attract those guests for many return visits. In a reservation management system you can create categories to track your guests' interests, as well as store specific notes that pertain to one individual guest. On their return visit, they will be pleasantly surprised at how well you remember them and their references. Storing such vital information helps build lasting customer relationships.

Question: What are the benefits of using web-based property management software?

Answer: I can think of several advantages in switching to a web-based program:

Security. The security and protection that a server can provide is above and beyond what a property owner would have time or resources to set up for their own computer. Back-ups are made constantly, firewalls are in place, and the server is monitored 24 hours a day and immediately alerts technicians in the case of any computer failure. While the thought of data being stored at a remote computer may seem 'risky', in reality their reservation information may be much more secure on the server than it is currently on their own desktop or network.

Worry-free updates. Of course I'd always like to be using the latest version of any software I purchase. With a web-based program, there is no need to purchase updates, or reconfigure a computer to be compatible with the latest version. A web-based software provider takes care of all the updates.

Question: Why is your software a good option?

Answer: Easy InnKeeping is an end to end reservation system. It is software designed with the Internet in mind. The Internet is increasingly becoming a source of new referrals for small accommodation properties. Linking the marketing power of the Internet with a software program like Easy InnKeeping, gives the property owner the ability to realise their marketing potential, while retaining control over their own room inventory. Offering availability information via the Internet is easily managed from the software program itself, which operates from your own PC. For those properties interested in real-time reservations via the Internet, this option is also available.

Online reservations with availability options

Why is it important to show availability information to Internet surfing guests? The Internet is a medium of information, and studies show that the more information your web site provides to the potential guest, the more likely they are to continue 'browsing' or 'visiting' your site. Answering the question: 'Do you have availability?' is often the first step towards making a reservation. You may wonder how to display this information on your site and keep it up to date. From within the software program, you can choose to display availability information on your web site and/or in large directories.

After guests search for availability, their reservation request is sent securely to the Easy InnKeeping software. You will receive an 'alert' that prompts you to check your 'inbox'. All reservation details are displayed – just click 'save' and email the confirmation.

Customisation

The developers of Easy InnKeeping realise that the B&B industry varies from one location to another and changes with the times. For properties that have very specific needs, Easy InnKeeping can be customised to fit so that it works for you.

To better understand the value of having your B&B online, for reservations, consider this: one third of Internet use today is travel related as more people use this medium to confirm their holiday plans and arrangements.

By displaying your Bed & Breakfast on a reservation system your property is made visible to potential guests from any part of the world. The beauty of online systems is twofold: Bed & Breakfast operators need not always be attending the phones, and travellers can have a confirmed reservation printed from their web browser without picking up the phone to make a call.

Online reservation networks normally charge either commissions or a flat fee for bookings made through the system.

GUEST REGISTRATION

Guests may not have any obligation to provide you with their permanent address, but we would suggest you ask for this, not least for the database you can then create to use for marketing at a later date.

Up until a few years ago an exercise book was sufficient for this purpose, but every year the level of professionalism in this industry is rising and it is this professionalism your guests will remember. They don't want to necessarily check in as if they were staying in a hotel, but an old exercise book is not really good enough.

So what are the options? There are two main forms of **registration**. One is the use of a **guest register** and the other is the individual **registration form** or card.

Guest register

This is a bound book, divided in columns, which your guests fill in on arrival.

Guests from overseas need to fill out the country of residence and passport number and, in some cases, their next destination. In this situation you will need to see your guest's passport.

In some regions there is a legal requirement for larger establishments to keep a record of the full name and nationality of all guests over the age of 16 years. Records in this situation must be kept for a minimum of 12 months. We suggest you contact your local authority for the legal requirements in your area.

The guest register is popular because all the details are in one place and in chronological order, making it easy for referral, and it is very inexpensive as each guest only takes up one line in the register. The downsides are that it can become tatty from overuse, illegible if guests make mistakes, and indiscreet, as your guests can easily see the personal details of other guests.

Individual registration form or card

The individual registration form or card performs the same functions as a register. It is more expensive than a register as each guest has an individual card or form, but you can generate these forms easily from your computer. This format is discreet as no one sees the form but you and your guest. It is neat, if a guest makes a mistake you can provide a new one and it can be filed easily. It also has space for both you and your guest to make comments (dietary, special needs, etc), which can be valuable information for later visits.

INSURANCE

Regardless of whether your business is in your home, on your property, around the corner, leased by you or a variation on these themes, insurance is one of the most important considerations you will have when running your Bed & Breakfast. It has the potential to protect your home and lifestyle in a way nothing else can – against the unexpected! After all, who can be properly prepared for the unexpected?

Insurance is a very simple concept. For an annual payment an insurance company agrees to provide specific cover for your **building and contents and other B&B specific areas, including liability to your paying guests.** Many insurers provide the facility to spread payments by direct debit but there is likely to be a charge for this.

Even if you believe you have adequate funds to replace or repair any loss that could occur, consideration must be given to investing in a suitable insurance policy.

In fact, in our increasingly litigious and varied society it would be irresponsible not to be adequately insured. Remember, as a host you have a responsibility not only to yourself and your family, but also to your guests. So what constitutes adequate insurance in your specific case? Remembering that one of the beauties of B&B is that they are all different from each other. Let us identify and evaluate the major areas of risk.

The biggest risk may be the general public themselves. You have people coming to your home or property you do not know and who do not know you. You can never guess how they look after their own possessions, so how can you know how they will look after yours?

Most B&B guests are the loveliest of people and some become life-long friends. Some, however, you will never please and you will wonder why they came in the first place. Things get broken perhaps, but no one confesses. Perhaps your lovely guest robes disappear after the guests leave. How do you handle situations like this and remain hospitable and content?

There are tricks of the trade concerning small losses and other operators will share some of these with you. Although your insurance policy should allow for claims of this nature, you may be penalised for making small claims continually. You need to realise that insurance companies are businesses as well. An insurer has the right to decline to renew a policy, or even quote in the first instance if they feel you are a bad risk, for example, if you make a lot of little claims on a continual basis.

Only you alone know your property intimately. Guests do not. In the dark, or in a strange place, people can get hurt. They don't know the stairs are a little uneven, or the coffee table is close to the sofa because the room is narrow. Perhaps they slip on a rug on the polished wooden floor, or in the night run into a piece of furniture or fall down the stairs. You will need to look at your property through the eyes of a stranger and try to determine any potential risks. This is called risk management.

You can protect yourself against these risks by taking out appropriate insurance coverage. The word 'appropriate' is important as many B&Bs pay for insurance each year, but don't have the cover they thought they had. Even worse, some do not have cover at all.

How can this be? Well, the first single most important thing to remember is that in most cases your current householders policy **will not cover you**. Be aware that many insurers do not insure B&Bs at all. This is not the negative it implies. If an insurance company doesn't understand what it is insuring, it is highly unlikely it will provide you with the type of policy you will require. If in doubt, ask questions.

One of the most important conditions of any policy is the duty of disclosure. For instance, your 'duty' would be to inform your current insurer once you decide to have paying guests or run a business from your home. This would also extend to long- or short-term paying students and to workers. You have an obligation to advise your insurance company of this and of any alterations you make to your home. Advising an insurance company in writing about the change from homeowner to B&B owner is imperative. It provides your insurers with accurate information and obliges them to confirm or decline your existing policy. Doing this in writing also provides some protection.

Firstly, you have a copy with details of when and to whom it was sent; secondly, written correspondence generally provokes a written response. This helps to protect you and substantiates basic information in the event of a dispute.

> **TIP**
>
> When writing to insurers be clear and specific and ask them for written confirmation for all areas of your cover, checking that you still have the elements needed from your domestic policy if you had one.

You will need to advise your insurer:

♦ The number of guests you have facilities for.

♦ What specific changes you might make to your home, for example renovations.

♦ Whether you have a restaurant, plan to serve morning or afternoon teas to guests or to the general public.

♦ Whether you will be serving or providing alcohol and any licences you may have that permit this.

♦ Whether you run any other business from your home or

property. Many householders' policies exclude the running of any business from their home.

◆ Whether you employ staff, perhaps a gardener or casual cleaning person. If you have a B&B and pay people to work for you, you are no longer a domestic situation and your domestic policy, if you have one, will not cover you.

◆ What sort of activities do you provide for your guests? Are you on a farm and have the guests interacting with farm animals or perhaps farm life?

Many insurers neither understand nor wish to insure B&B accommodation and will tell you that quite clearly. Some may offer separate liability policies. That may solve one aspect of your insurance needs, but what does it mean for your building and contents cover?

Perhaps they offer to cover your home under a combined domestic and business policy. This can leave building and contents with very different, and usually less cover than the cover you have enjoyed under a householder's policy.

This combined type of insurance cover requires you to pick and choose each section of cover, for example, glass, fire, money, burglary and then pay extra for basic covers that would be automatically included in a specialist B&B policy. Buying separate liability policies is expensive and can mean you have two or three different insurance companies covering your needs. If something happens, are these providers easily able to work together or will there be problems determining who is responsible for what because of the mishmash of policies put together like a patchwork quilt? You are also likely to have an excess (deductible) under each policy – whereas only one excess is likely to apply if you have a specialist policy.

If you have a farm and already have one or other of these policies, *do not* assume it extends to your B&B as well. It probably won't, unless you have specifically arranged for it to do so.

What cover do I need to I consider?

Public liability – relates to the general public in a business sense. It relates to injury and property damage caused by your personal negligence and/or business negligence. If part of your property is not well maintained and clear of debris, a guest may fall and sustain an injury (where you are proven to have been negligent – this also covers the cost of defending such claims).

Product liability – is in relation to any products you provide, but is especially relevant to the food you serve. It doesn't matter whether you bought it from the bakery or not, should a guest find something 'extra' in it you are liable.

Employers' liability – once you know that you are going to employ staff, whether full time, part time or casual cleaners, chefs or gardeners, talk with your insurance broker in detail about employers' liability insurance. This is compulsory in the UK and may be automatically covered by your home insurance.

Buildings and contents cover – Your building and contents insurance should reflect true replacement values. If you have more than one building it is advisable you show each building and the contents of each separately. Insurance is not based on a market value or saleable value. It is based on replacing or repairing. Therefore if you are unsure it is wise to ask a builder or valuer to provide you with an estimate based on your property. Add to that a percentage or lump sum allowance for removal of debris, architect's fees and council requirements, etc. Please bear in mind the building regulations applicable to listed properties. You should pay particular attention to ensuring that you have adequate cover.

It is possible to obtain an indication of the rebuilding cost of your property from the web site run by the Association of British Insurers (see www.abi.org.uk). There is a link under the 'consumer' section.

Insurers will be interested in the construction of your property. Usually standard construction is considered to be homes built from brick, stone, slate or tile. If your property is built from other materials then please notify the insurer. You should also say if any part of it has a flat roof.

Be aware that you should discuss with your builder any requirements for covering work carried out, should you need to repair or renovate. The best way to protect yourself in this respect is to employ a well known builder with a good reputation. He should carry his own insurance and be happy to show evidence of this to you.

Most buildings policies will also cover the cost of alternative accommodation for the policyholder and their family whilst the main premises is not habitable. The level of cover does vary but this could prove to be an important aspect of cover in the event of a major loss.

Other factors to consider are security, favourable rates may apply if you have door and window locks of a certain standard.

All policies will include a 'un-occupancy period' of usually 30 to 45 days. If your property is likely to remain empty for this period of time be aware that the cover will be substantially reduced after this period. This may be relevant to those of you who over winter in Europe.

When assessing your contents cover, have special regard for antiques, valuables and other high risk portable items such as cameras, laptops and jewellery. Some insurers may ask you to improve the security of your home (for example by fitting a safe), if these items form a high proportion of your overall cover. It is a good idea to collate a list of these and keep photographic evidence/receipts for any valued over £1,500/€2,192.

Alternative accommodation and rent – this section is likely to be a benefit of a specialist B&B policy. It will cover the additional costs you incur for alternative accommodation whilst your home is uninhabitable following a major loss. The amount of cover provided is usually expressed as a percentage of the contents sum insured but is typically around £10,000/€14,613.

Loss of board and lodgings – this will compensate you for loss of income for pre-booked accommodation up to a maximum amount of say £6,000/€8,768.

Guests' effects cover – cover for your guests' belongings.

Business equipment – e.g. fax machine, computer etc.

Goods in transit – e.g. food and drink while in transport from the suppliers to your premises.

Money – cover for cash kept on your premises.

Keys – cover for theft or loss of keys.

Full theft cover – most standard household policies will exclude theft unless by forcible and violent entry.

Full accidental damage cover – your insurer must not be able to come back to you when you want to claim for a broken window or a cracked hand basin and say, 'prove to us a guest did not do it!'

Personal possessions cover – the personal possessions section (also known as all risks) will cover your family's portable valuable items outside of the home, and in many cases whilst travelling overseas. Do not overlook this aspect of cover.

Some policies will also include legal and home emergency helplines. The former may just provide advice on legal or contractual disputes, but nonetheless can be an important source of information. The home emergency line can be invaluable in locating tradesman 24 hours a day, particularly in an emergency. The insurers often operate panels of such people who they have previously vetted and who offer guarantees of service in return for regular work.

There are very few insurance companies who provide a B&B specific policy. Those who do generally provide this through an insurance broker. In the main, you will find this specialised cover is available as a specific scheme managed by that broker.

Don't rely on your current insurance broker to find one for you.
The best place to find out about these people is through a referral
from another B&B, your regional tourist board or from one of
the B&B associations. Try using a search engine on the Internet
by typing in the phrase 'Bed & Breakfast insurance', to locate
B&B insurance providers.

These insurers will still have differences between the coverage they
offer and their service and involvement in the industry, but it will
be specific to the B&B industry. Don't be afraid to get different
quotes and ask as many questions as you can. This allows you to
make informed decisions and buy as directly as possible.

You should also be aware of paying for expensive 'hotel'
insurance policies. They may give much wider and higher cover
limits, but why pay more for cover that you do not need, e.g.
neon signs, loss of liquor licence.

What additional cover should I consider?

Business interruption – If you do not have a specialist 'package'
policy, which automatically includes this form of cover, you
should seriously consider it. Following physical loss or damage to
your property, there could be an interruption to your business. A
serious fire, for example, may prevent you from opening your
establishment to paying guests until the property has been rebuilt,
redecorated and refurbished. In the meantime you will lose
income but will still have to meet continuing overheads. If you
rely upon the income from your B&B to live, it is essential that
you have this cover.

For a claim to be met, the property must have been damaged by
an insured peril. Any saving in expenses, such as food and

cleaning costs, will be deducted from the amount of the claim.

You should ensure that your indemnity period is sufficient to cover your loss of gross profit until you have managed to rebuild your trade to the same level you were achieving prior to the loss. A minimum period of 12 months is recommended but for some properties (such as listed buildings), rebuilding may take considerably longer and a greater indemnity period therefore needs to be selected.

Motor vehicle insurance – Motor vehicles should be insured according to your insurer's criteria. Let them advise you how their policy works and how your business activity will be interpreted by them.

Many insurers will provide a car for business use by the policyholder and/or their spouse for a small additional cost. However, if employees will also use the car for business, including picking up guests, this will result in a more significant increase in premium.

If you insure your vehicle for business use you may be able to claim for a percentage of the premium under your tax. You should discuss your plans with your insurer.

Personal accident and sickness/income protection – If you have enjoyed personal accident and sickness/income protection whilst in a position outside of the B&B, please keep it going. As we get older, it becomes more difficult to obtain this type of insurance. Once again, your specialists in B&B insurance will know what options they have available for you.

Find out about your insurance. It's best not to guess – Don't be afraid to ask questions about your existing insurance, or quotes that you obtain. Let the experts do what they do best and let them know what sorts of things concern you and just exactly what items you want to cover.

What you choose to insure, with whom, and to what value is up to you. Make informed decisions, ask questions, take your time and get it right. Remember that it is a small price to pay if something bad does happen and you will sleep as soundly as your guests – free of worry and confident in your insurance broker and your insurance policy, if you have taken the time to do it right.

Ryan Insurance Group specialise in providing one complete solution to your B&B insurance needs, their contact details can be found under Useful Addresses at the back of the book.

PAYMENT
There is no set way of handling this part of your interaction with your guests. Some B&Bs prefer to settle the account at the beginning of the stay, particularly if you do not have extras that the guest can choose during their stay, while others keep to the traditional way of paying at the end. It is your establishment – the way you run it is up to you.

Either way, you will need to present your guest with an **itemised account**, retaining a duplicate yourself. This could be in the form of a handwritten invoice, which you can buy from your local stationers, or a computer generated account on your letterhead where you can store your record on disk.

METHODS OF PAYMENT

There are many different options for payment and you will need to decide which you will choose to accept. You might like to discuss your options and the positives and negatives of each with your financial adviser and bank manager. It is a good idea to show your payment options on your promotional literature.

Cash

This is the best option for any business because of the cleared funds aspect to **cash**. The only negatives are that you may be charged a small deposit fee and you will need a safe to store the money until you can go to the bank.

Cheques

Many establishments choose not to accept **cheques**, however, many of your guests will expect this facility. Some guests may wish to pay by personal cheque either in local currency or in foreign currency. If you accept cheques in foreign currency make sure the amount on the cheque covers the costs of converting the cheque into local currency.

This method of payment is not recommended because personal cheques can be 'stopped' or 'returned' for varying reasons. If a personal cheque is returned it will mean that you the B&B owner would be out of pocket for the duration of the stay that the payment originally covered. If you do accept cheques, then be sure to view the guest's cheque guarantee card or driver's licence and record the guest's details on the reverse side of the cheque. Ensure any alterations are initialled and the cheque is not post-dated.

With the spread of cash machines it is reasonable to assume that cash or credit card usage will be the favoured method of payment.

Credit and debit cards

The financial size of your establishment will probably make the difference as to whether or not you choose to accept **credit** or **debit cards**. Many of your guests will want to settle their account by this method as this is the payment revolution of the 21st century. We use it to access our accounts to pay for petrol, groceries, pharmaceuticals, in fact almost everything you can think of.

If you choose to go down this route there are a few things you will need to do. Firstly you need to apply for merchant card status from your bank. For the privilege of using their service you will pay a commission of around 2% of the face value of the payment. You will be given a floor limit, which usually equates to the charge of your cheapest night. Any charge after that will require an authorisation number. When applying for merchant card status be sure to have a telephone facility. This will allow you to take a non-refundable deposit. The hardware required is multi-functional in that it accepts both credit and debit card transactions.

It works via modem-based technology. The set up costs, excluding the multi-functional hardware, could be quite expensive, but is worthwhile if your property is a large guest house. Talk to your bank manager about the costs.

Traveller's cheques

Overseas guests are the most likely to use this form of 'currency' instead of credit or debit cards.

If in English pounds or euros it is as good as cash, but **traveller's cheques** in foreign currency will require you to convert and to add the conversion service fee the bank will charge you. This can be quite problematic because your bank must be comfortable accepting and negotiating third party cheques, and this could be costly. Again, discuss this type of payment with your bank manager first. You will need to ensure the traveller produces suitable identification, e.g. a passport, and signs the cheque in front of you.

Foreign currency

If you choose to accept this you will need to convert the **foreign currency** into your country's currency and add the service fee the bank will charge you. Be aware that banks factor in a 4 to 5% margin, plus a fee for accepting and converting foreign currency. You must ensure you get the exchange rate from your bank. Get the money to the bank that day, otherwise you may lose money on the transaction if the exchange rate changes. Try to encourage your guests to change the money themselves.

Online payment solutions

PayPal has a program that enables anyone with an email address to easily send and receive secure payments online. PayPal is an eBay company, specialising in online payment solutions with more than 86 million account members worldwide. They operate in 56 countries and support six currencies – Australian dollars, euros, US dollars, pounds sterling, Canadian dollars and Japanese yen. They claim that their program uses very good commercially available encryption technology to ensure that all financial information is never shared with buyers or sellers.

Pre-paid vouchers

One form of payment, which you may have to think about, is the **pre-paid voucher**. Many tour operators and other agencies issue these to their clients who then hand them to their B&B host in exchange for a night's stay. The accommodation may be pre-booked for an additional fee, or on a go-as-you please basis.

This arrangement has to be formally agreed months in advance. The B&B host normally posts the voucher to a local agency, acting on behalf of the company which issued them. Systems can vary from company to company and there are usually additional agreements about supplements for extras of one kind or another such as children sharing 'superior accommodation', which must be paid directly to the host by the guest on the spot.

You may be approached individually about this type of business or it could be one of the many options open to you as a member of a consortium or B&B association. Either way you should discuss it fully with others already in the system before committing yourself. There is normally no cost involved for those agreeing to participate in voucher transactions. However, there may be a commission payable at some stage in the process. Check with your voucher issuer for their procedure.

Travel agents are encouraging clients to purchase pre-paid accommodation vouchers before they leave home. This has resulted in an increase in the use of vouchers. The B&B voucher business is big and growing, especially where the Bed & Breakfast hosts are well organised and belong to their own associations. This is particularly the case throughout Ireland where a truly vast B&B voucher business has been painstakingly built up and finely tuned over the past 30 years or so.

The flexibility of B&B voucher programmes is very appealing to international visitors travelling around the UK and Ireland. Discover Travel & Tours is very well known within the international travel trade and is always looking for quality B&Bs, inns and guest houses to join their programme – see their contact details under the 'pre-paid voucher' heading in the Useful Addresses section.

FINANCIAL RECORDS

You need to keep records of your Bed & Breakfast's financial performance primarily for taxation purposes, but also to help monitor your business's growth. **VAT records** are required to be kept by all registered business operators. As we have said many times in this publication, it would be wise to contact a financial adviser prior to deciding anything to do with your Bed & Breakfast. The HM Revenue & Customs office particularly, is a fount of information. You are legally required to keep your records for taxation purposes and the tax office has a CD-ROM designed for this purpose.

Sage, or a similar computer record-keeping program, is another worthwhile investment for record keeping and for tracking your business activities. Due to the complexities of tax systems, we will not be going in to great depth on the records the government requires you to keep.

Other than recommending that you contact HM Revenue & Customs we would suggest you apply to your closest VAT office for registration if required. HM Revenue & Customs administer this office. VAT registered business must show a nine-digit VAT number on all literature and documentation pertaining to the business. As for the figures you need to assess your financial progress, we would suggest that every month you reconcile and look at the following:

Accommodation cash flow

This is the permanent record of your occupancy and income. With this information you can compare month-to-month, year-to-year trading, highlighting regular seasonal highs and lows and allowing you to forecast accurately. You can then turn this information into graphs, perhaps even comparing weekend and weekday trade, to plan for the coming year or season. As months go by you will be able to make decisions on when your busiest periods are, enabling you to market to fill in the gaps or even the best time for you to take a well-earned break.

Operating expenses

These are the fixed costs each month, such as leases, rent, rates, insurance, loans, memberships, etc, plus your variable costs, such as telephone, electricity, gas, water, labour (including your own), food, decoration, etc. Again, graphs are a great tool for comparison and can help determine whether further investigation is needed.

For example, one month you may have spent £300 or €250 on food, while the next you only spent £210 or €180, but your accommodation receipts were similar. Ask yourself what changed.

Break-even analysis

The combination of your operating expenses and your accommodation cash flow provides you with the material to prepare a **break-even analysis**. When your costs are higher than your income you are running at a loss. Break-even is the point when the two meet, and all income above that is profit.

Bank balances

Another long-term indicator is the comparison between your opening and closing **bank balance** each month. It helps track your expenditure and is also good to convert to graph form.

Debtors and creditors

Monthly reconciliation of the money owed to you by **debtors**, and by you to **creditors**, is imperative when running a successful business. Ensure that you pay by your due date, as you want to maintain a good credit rating, particularly if you are part of a small community.

You should put in place a process to follow up debtors. While they are not paying you, you are losing valuable interest.

Profit and loss statement

This is the conclusion of all of the above. Subtracting your costs from actual sales revenue from accommodation receipts will give you a gross profit estimate for the month. Then subtract all other costs including a pro rata amount for variable expenditure. This will give you a net profit figure.

The net profit is the bottom line figure from which you can draw cash, pay off capital or retain cash in the business for future growth. It is also the figure you can match against the value of your business assets to see the return on your investments.

With all these figures at your fingertips you can build an accurate picture of the financial position of your business. Recording these figures each month gives you the ability to keep your business finely tuned. You will be able to see trends in profits, costs and sales. It will also help you to see any potential problems if one or more of these indicators begin to go off track.

A business will eventually fail if it is not profitable. It may also fail (even if it is profitable on paper) when cash flow is not monitored to ensure that debits are paid when due or you take too much cash out of the business.

General ledger

A general ledger is a day-by-day record of your daily incomings and outgoings. In any business, including B&Bs, you need to ensure a general ledger is established and maintained in order to monitor debits and credits against each salient item. An accountant or financial adviser is the best person to assist you in setting up your books, in particular your general ledger. Again, a suitable commercial program can help you here.

BANKING

It is imperative that you put your payments into the bank as quickly as possible, for both security and financial reasons. If you are unable to get to your bank every day, and have the potential to carry large sums of money on your premises, you must inform your insurance company. We would also suggest the installation of a small safe.

A meeting with your bank manager would be a good idea when starting up your business. Your bank should be able to advise you of the best bank accounts to run your business and will provide you with the necessary documentation that will need to accompany any transaction.

To make your time at the bank more efficient:

◆ Always sort coins and notes into denominations and place coins in the bags provided by the bank.

- List your cheques on the deposit slip.
- Pay your foreign currency to the bank using a separate slip.

Don't forget that for credit card transactions there is nothing to bank as the payments are electronic. Debit card transactions are straight through into your account.

If you are unable to get to the bank during trading hours, find out if the bank has a **night safe facility**. The bank will be able to issue you with a commercial wallet in which to put your money. The bank will also give you a key or a code that will unlock the night safe.

12

The Hospitality Industry and You

The important thing to remember as you start this journey is that you are not alone. You are part of a larger entity called the hospitality industry. Much of your success will be your ability to work co-operatively with others in the industry both here and overseas.

THE STRUCTURE OF TOURISM AUTHORITIES

Each nation's government has its respective **tourism authority** that, in essence, takes responsibility to develop strategies that ensure their share of tourist revenue.

The United Kingdom has four tourist boards: VisitBritain (formerly the English Tourism Council and the British Tourist Authority), VisitScotland (formerly the Scottish Tourist Board), the Northern Ireland Tourist Board and VisitWales (formerly the Wales Tourist Board).

The British Tourist Authority (BTA) and the English Tourism Council (formerly the English Tourist Board), which have now been merged to form VisitBritain, VisitScotland and VisitWales were set up under the Development of Tourism Act in 1969 (the Northern Ireland Tourist Board was set up under separate legislation). The Act's aim was to co-ordinate the diverse interests that make up the tourism industry and provide it with a single voice.

VisitBritain reports to the Department for Culture, Media and Sport (DCMS).

VisitWales reports to the National Assembly for Wales.

VisitScotland reports to the Scottish Executive.

VisitBritain works in partnership with Britain's national and regional tourist boards and delivery partners.

The regional tourist boards deliver many of their services through localised tourism bodies, which we suggest you log into, for those registered with their local tourist association may well find they get the majority of their bookings from this source, either by direct bookings through the association or by referring to their official publication.

For the reasons mentioned above, we urge everyone in the Bed & Breakfast industry to join their respective tourism organisation, board or association. In some places, some form of membership is compulsory. This will help you identify why tourists visit your area, to network with other B&B operators, to access local information that helps you make better target market decisions and keeps you up to date with tourism development. Be proactive not reactive and join your association.

A publicly owned company called Tourism Ireland Limited (TIL), has been established by agreement between Bord Fáilte and the Northern Ireland Tourism Board to provide the following two main services:

◆ To increase tourism to the whole of Ireland.
◆ To support Northern Ireland to realise its tourism potential.

See Useful Addresses for a list of tourism structures and membership entry levels plus other valuable industry contacts.

LOCAL TOURIST ORGANISATIONS

If you have not yet got the picture that you need to be actively involved in the tourism community, we have failed. Your local tourism authority is probably the most important organisation you can join. It will provide you with vital information about your market, but most importantly it will give you vital contacts. Local tourism operators thrive off interaction with each other. It really is a case of you scratch my back and I'll scratch yours.

Destination marketing plays an integral part in the marketing of tourism products. Whether the product is an attraction, activity, scenery, or a Bed & Breakfast, they all, collectively, form the essence of the destination. The more popular the destination, the better are the chances for individual tourism operators to promote and sell their products to potential customers in a cost-effective way.

Destination marketing, promoting the unique brand of a destination, is one of the tasks local or regional tourism organisations are charged with. They prepare the base from which individual operators can undertake their own marketing and promotion at a reduced cost.

Locations such as Lucca, Sienna or Firenze, may not mean a lot to many people, nor would they necessarily associate them with any type of holiday experience. Mention the destination brand, Tuscany, and the story is different. Many will associate that brand not only with a very specific holiday expectation, but they can also place it geographically. In other words, if the destination is known in the marketplace or if it has brand identity, each individual business has the chance of being seen in its marketplace and to reach potential customers faster and at a lesser cost.

It should be in everyone's interest, from the smallest B&B operator, to the largest attraction, to ensure that your local and regional tourism organisations receive sufficient support to undertake destination marketing, promote the region and create brand awareness. In return, individual businesses will benefit.

B&B CLASSIFICATION
There is a new **national accommodation classification scheme** that is supported by VisitBritain, VisitScotland, the Wales Tourist Board, the AA and the RAC that came into being in January 2006.

All organisations involved are using the developed and agreed to, common standard requirements to determine the Star rating of your property. You can choose which of the mentioned organisations you want to assess your property but do understand, that they will all be the same Star rating.

There is a minimum entry requirement for achieving a **One Star** rating:

- A cooked breakfast, or substantial continental one.

- Owners/staff must be available for guest arrivals and departures and also meal times i.e. breakfast.

- Once registered, guests must have free access to your property at all times unless you have made other entry arrangements with your guests.

- All serviced areas must be kept clean and maintained (minimum quality requirement) as well as facilities and the delivery of services.

- A dining room or similar eating area is available unless meals are served in the bedrooms.

- You must meet all current statutory obligations and provide public liability cover.

The key requirements at rating levels are as follows:

Three Star and above
- Access to both sides of all beds for double occupancy.
- Bathrooms/shower cannot be shared with the owner.
- From January 2008, a washbasin in every guest bedroom (could be en suite or bathroom).

Four Star
- From January 2008 at least 50% of guest rooms to have an en suite or private facilities.

Five Star

◆ All guest bedrooms to have an en suite or with private facilities (from January 2008).

As agreed to by all assessor agencies, those wishing to obtain a higher Star level will need to provide enhanced quality standards across all areas with a particular emphasis on cleanliness, breakfast, hospitality, bedrooms and bathrooms.

Definitions set down by the grading authorities are:

Bed & Breakfast	Accommodation in a private house, run by the owner and no more than six paying guests.
Guest house	Accommodation provided for more than six paying guests and run on a more commercial basis than a B&B. Usually more services, for example, dinner is provided by the owners.
Farmstay	B&B or guest house accommodation provided on a working farm or smallholding.

Statutory obligations

All statutory obligations must be adhered to and include the following:

◆ fire precautions
◆ price display orders
◆ food/safety/hygiene
◆ licensing
◆ health and safety
◆ anti-discrimination
◆ trade descriptions

- data protection
- Hotel Proprietors Act.

You will also be asked to show clear evidence that public liability cover is being maintained and that the above requirements are fulfilled.

We strongly suggest that all readers choose a grading organisation and click onto their web site, and download the pdf file on this new grading format, as it impacts on how you prepare your property for Bed & Breakfast purposes.

So why should you be classified? As more people enter this market the guest is going to become more discerning. Those properties that can advertise their rating will only benefit from it.

Tourism accreditation is a process designed to establish and continually improve industry standards for conducting tourism businesses. It aims to assist every tourism business to improve the way it operates.

It is important to bear in mind that the Star grade takes into account the nature of the property and the expectation of the guests – so a farmhouse is just as entitled to five Stars as a country hotel, as long as what it offers is of the highest standard.

☆	Fair and acceptable
☆☆	Good
☆☆	Very good
☆☆☆	Excellent[*]
☆☆☆☆	Exceptional, world-class[*]

*You will be guaranteed a wider range of equipment.

SYMBOLS

Below is a guide to the **symbols** used to indicate the features and facilities available for all the farms listed in tourism guides.

Symbol	Accommodation type
	Bed & Breakfast
	Self catering
	Bunkhouse
	Camping
	Caravanning

Symbol	Explanation
	Children welcome (minimum age)
	Dogs by arrangement
	Accommodation for disabled/less able people – check for details
	No smoking
	Smokers welcome
	Credit cards accepted
	Business people welcome
	Way marked walks on farm
	Foreign languages spoken
	Riding on farm
	Fishing on farm
CH	Country house, not a working farm

A rating from one star to five stars is the best way for guests to assess the quality of stay that they are looking at. Ratings are an internationally applied yardstick and are administered in this country according to very strict guidelines.

B&B/Farmstay associations

Most nations have a Bed & Breakfast farmstay association that is recognised by the public and tourism bodies as the peer group for this accommodation sector. Their prime role is to represent

> **TIP**
> Being graded gives you an advantage over your competitors.

the interests of B&B farmstay operators in both government and tourism circles. Another area they tend to focus on is training programs that assist the operators in being more professional when going about their business.

Most associations have a good web site that is often linked to either a B&B/farmstay guide or to an online reservation switch. You can find some contact details under Useful Addresses at the back of this book.

13

Marketing Your B&B

This chapter will help you to design an effective **marketing plan** or concept, for your Bed & Breakfast. It should help you come to decisions on what style of marketing (advertising, promotions, public relations, direct mail, etc.) will suit both your customer and your financial situation.

MARKETING CONCEPT

The underpinning factor of your **marketing concept** rests on the importance of guests to your Bed & Breakfast. All of your activities should be aimed at satisfying your guests' needs, while obtaining a profitable, rather than maximum, occupancy.

To develop a marketing concept for your Bed & Breakfast you must:

◆ Determine the needs of your guests (market research).
◆ Develop competitive advantages (marketing strategy).
◆ Select specific markets to serve (target marketing).
◆ Determine how to satisfy those needs (marketing mix).

MARKET RESEARCH

The fundamentals of operating a successful Bed & Breakfast are the same as running any small business. If you do your homework first then there is less likelihood of coming unstuck.

The aim of **market research** is to find out who your guests are, what they want, where and when they want it.

> **TIP**
>
> Ongoing research is a prerequisite for ongoing viability.

This research can also expose problems in the way in which you provide products or services, and find areas for expansion of current services to fill customer demand. Market research should also identify trends that can affect bookings and profit levels.

Market research should give you more information than simply who your customers are. Use this knowledge to determine matters such as your market share, the effectiveness of your advertising and promotions, and the response to any new value added services that you have introduced.

While larger companies hire professionals to do their research, small business owners and managers are closer to their customers and are able to learn much faster the likes and dislikes of their guests. They are better positioned to react quickly to any change in customer preferences.

What to look for

On the basis that you have identified your initial target market, the market research required should investigate four distinct areas:

- customers
- customer needs
- competition
- trends.

Some of the things you might like to look at are as follows:

Customer (demographics)
- Age.
- Income.
- Occupation.
- Family size.
- Marital status.
- Country of residence.
- Interests and hobbies.

Customer needs
- Rest and relaxation?
- Is their stay for a limited time, for example, conference?
- Will guests come frequently, for example, business travellers or for sight-seeing?
- Are guests looking for a wider experience in your geographical location?

Competition
- What is the competition's market share?
- How much revenue do you suspect they make?
- How many Bed & Breakfasts are targeting the same market?
- What attracts customers to them?
- What strengths do they advertise?

Trends
- Any population shifts.
- Changes in local tourism development.

- Life-style changes in the nearest metro city area.
- Short-break holidays taken during the week instead of only at weekends.

Where to get information
There are two general sources of information: data already available, and data that can be collected progressively by the Bed & Breakfast operator. The following sources may provide already accessible data.

- The business section of any well-run public library.
- Tourism authorities/local associations.
- Commerce and/or traders' group.
- Professional market research services.

Data can be obtained by the Bed & Breakfast's own research efforts:

- Telephone surveys.
- Local and national newspapers.
- Surveys sent by mail.
- Questionnaires.
- Guest service cards.

Market research does not have to be sophisticated and expensive. While money can be spent in collecting research material, a lot of valuable information can be accessed by the Bed & Breakfast operator using the following methods.

Employees
This is one of the best sources of information about guests' likes and dislikes. Usually employees work more directly

with guests and hear complaints that may not make it to the owner. They are also aware of items or services that guests may request, and that the Bed & Breakfast doesn't currently offer.

Guests
Talk to your guests to get a feel for your clientele, and ask them where improvements can be made. Collecting guest comments and suggestions is an effective form of research, as well as instilling customer confidence in your product and property.

Competition
Monitoring the competition can be a useful source of information. Their activities may provide important information about guest demands that were overlooked. They may be capturing part of the market by offering something unique or different. Likewise, Bed & Breakfast operators can capitalise on unique points of their product that the competition does not offer.

Records and files
Looking at your business records and files can be very informative. Peruse your revenue records, complaints, receipts or any other records that can show you where your guests live or work, or how and what interests them. One Bed & Breakfast operator found that addresses on cash receipts enabled the pinpointing of guests in a specific geographic area. She thought clients may like to sample the similar, yet different features her area offered.

With this kind of information one can cross reference the guest addresses and check the effectiveness of the advertising placements. You need to take into account that this material represents the past and the information that you need to determine present and future trends may mean that some past information is too obsolete to be effective, but at least you will have a general idea of what to look for.

MARKETING STRATEGY

With the research information gathered, the next step is to develop a marketing strategy. Use this information to determine areas where the competition doesn't adequately fill consumer demand, or to find areas where a new service or different promotion would capture part of the market. A new Bed & Breakfast may capture a significant market share by aiming its marketing strategy on areas not focused on by the competition.

Some examples of the various areas of emphasis include offering:

- More innovative sightseeing options.
- Better value for the guests, for example an emphasis on quality.
- Specialised service instead of a broad one.
- Modified facilities, or any improvements.
- A more flexible pricing policy.

While a new Bed & Breakfast can enter this business and capture a share of the market, an established one can use the same strategies to increase its market share.

TARGET MARKETING

Once your marketing strategy is developed, you need to determine with which customer group this would be most effective. For example, a 'value for

TIP
Find ways to fill rooms out of season. Put together packages with other products suppliers.

money' option may be appealing to the family market while 'quality and top service' would be more attractive to couples.

Another example could be offering a gift voucher that is set at a fixed denomination i.e. €100/£100. The person who buys a pre-paid voucher might present it to a friend or family member as a gift. This allows the holder to use the voucher as payment when checking into your Bed & Breakfast.

Remember that different market strategies may appeal to different target markets. Apply the collected data to choose the combinations that will work best.

The market is defined by different segments. Some examples of this are as follows.

Geographic
Specialise product options to suit guests who live in certain neighbourhoods or regions, or who are from different climates.

Demographic
Direct advertising to families, retired people, the disadvantaged, or to the occupation or profession of potential guests.

Special interest groups
Target promotions to the opinions or attitudes of the customers (political or religious, for example).

Product benefits
Aim marketing to emphasise the benefits of the product or service that would appeal to consumers who holiday for this reason (low cost or easy access).

Previous guests
Identify and promote to those guests who have stayed before.

THE MARKETING MIX
Before the marketing mix decision is made, determine what
purpose these marketing efforts are going to serve. Are they to:

- decpen the customer base;
- increase market share;
- increase revenue;
- reach new geographic markets; or
- to increase occupancy?

After these objectives are established, determine a date for
accomplishing these objectives. The marketing mix allows the Bed
& Breakfast to combine different marketing decision areas such
as services, promotion and advertising, pricing and place, to
construct an overall marketing programme.

PRODUCTS AND SERVICES
Use the product or service itself as a marketing resource. Having
something unique provides motivation behind advertising. While
the ideas mentioned under market strategy apply here, another
option is to change or modify the
service. Additional attention may be
given to a product if it has changed
colour, size or style, while a service may
draw similar attention by modifying the
services provided. Remember sales and promotional opportunities
are generated by product differentiation.

> **TIP**
> Provide the service you
> advertise.

PROMOTION AND ADVERTISING
With a marketing strategy and clear objectives outlined, use

advertising to get the message out to the customers. Advertising can be through:

- the *Yellow* or *Golden Pages*
- a press release
- the newspaper
- billboards and posters
- B&B guide books
- local tourism publications
- direct mail.

The Internet is a relatively cheap way to promote your B&B both domestically and overseas and should now be considered the centrepiece of your overall marketing strategy.

One reason to advertise is to highlight promotional activities. This will serve to both highlight your property and offer added incentive for customer patronage. For example you may wish to promote:

TIP

Invite local tourist information staff to visit. Give them a complimentary night's stay so they can experience what you have to offer. This can effectively sell your B&B.

- midweek, two nights for the price of one offers
- coupons or gift vouchers
- special activities, e.g., mystery-solving evenings.

The aim is to try to reach the largest number of people with the money allocated to advertising and promotion. This may be accomplished by using several different methods of advertising. Be creative and implement ideas.

Advertising material

The following are some ideas that could help increase the response from your advertising material. Good quality advertising can be costly, but very rewarding. Again, the emphasis is on 'good'. It's also worth considering full-page advertisements (particularly if you are targeting the luxury market), but *after* your first year of profitable trade. It is not always appropriate to spend large sums of money in your first year, especially in expensive, national travel magazines, as people don't tend to keep them, and you will have other priorities for your marketing budget.

Always write the headline from your guests' point of view not your own

People tend to not look at their products and services from the perspective of the people buying them. The sooner your prospective guests recognise themselves and their own wants and needs in the words you use in your headline, the faster they will respond.

Use the words 'You', 'New' and/or 'How to' in your headline

These are proven words that capture attention. Connect them to a benefit your prospective guests may want or need, and the response will increase.

Make your opening sentence continue what you were talking about in the headline

If in your headline you promised your prospective guest a relaxing stay in your Bed & Breakfast, then say something in your opening sentence about this to get them even more excited about staying with you.

Tell your whole story, in miniature by the time the first paragraph is over.

People have a very short attention span. Try to telescope your entire story down to a sound bite in writing. Think of how they do this on the TV news, where they give you the key points of an item and then say 'more at 11'. Far more people will read your copy, and the results should produce bookings. Use the rest of your copy to retell your story, in more detail.

Use specific, powerful and true testimonials

No matter how honest or persuasive you are, people usually won't believe everything or take everything in as being possible when they first read your copy.

They need to get to know and trust you. That can take some time, but unfortunately you don't want to wait. You have to persuade them right now. They will be much more likely to believe what you say when other people are singing your praises. Include testimonials to enhance your credibility.

TIP

Always have a book of photographs and transparencies for unexpected visiting guests.

Edit your copy ruthlessly

If a word doesn't keep the reader's attention by making your copy more interesting, or what you are selling seem more appealing, cut it out.

Copywriting is the art of doing more with fewer words. Every word has to work really hard, and your copy has to be easy to read.

MARKETING PERFORMANCE

After the marketing mix decision is implemented, the next step is to evaluate performance. With a detailed list of your objectives, monitor how well the decisions are developing.

- ◆ Evaluate objectives such as:
  - *Market share.* Has the increased share been reached?
  - *Revenue volume.* Was the increase achieved?
  - *Strategy.* Did the combinations of target markets and strategy work effectively? Which ones didn't?

- ◆ You should also evaluate the following decisions:
  - Did the advertising efforts reach target groups?
  - Were promotions timely?
  - Did customers respond to specials, coupons or other incentives?

- ◆ Additionally, consider the following:
  - Is your Bed & Breakfast doing all it can to satisfy the guest?
  - Is it easy for customers to find what they want at a competitive price?
  - If these objectives were not reached, what were the reasons?
  - If they worked well, what elements were most effective?

By evaluating performance after decisions have been made, there is reference for future decision-making, based on past results. In addition, periodically assess customer feelings and opinions toward your Bed & Breakfast and how well your guests' needs are being satisfied. This can be done through surveys, customer comments cards, or simply by asking them, 'How did you enjoy your stay?'

Assessing performance and asking for customer input brings around market research again. Your marketing plan is a continuous effort to identify and adapt to changes in markets, customer taste, and the economy for the success of your Bed & Breakfast.

PUBLIC RELATIONS

All B&Bs have certain things in common: if nothing else you are all dealing with people who are away from their home. Understanding what Bed & Breakfasts have to offer, and the people who patronise them, will play an important part in your marketing approach.

You can quite safely say people frequent Bed & Breakfasts for:

◆ the personal, pampered feeling they offer;
◆ the safety and security offered by smaller establishments;
◆ the opportunity for closer interaction with local surroundings; and
◆ their suitability for short holiday breaks.

Taking these factors into account you could very well find that public relations could offer your Bed & Breakfast your cheapest and most effective form of promotion.

Media relations, where you try to influence journalists and producers of newspapers, magazines, radio shows and TV programmes to do a story on your Bed & Breakfast, at little or no cost, is likely to be the most relevant sector of the PR market. Editorial, as we call this coverage, has more credibility than paid advertising and gives an opportunity to cover more facts.

A media kit is the introduction, story, photographs and any other appropriate materials, such as brochures, which you send to the media. The most important component of the kit is the story, or the press release. Used well, a series of press releases can keep your establishment 'in the news'.

Look not only at promoting yourself, but also the attractions of your area, offering your Bed & Breakfast as the most convenient place to stay.

Media releases

Following are some rules to observe when preparing a press release.

Write your story considering the questions, 'Who?, What?, Why? When?, Where? and How? This will help you to include all relevant information.

You must remain focused on what your story is and ensure it appears different from all the other media kits that appear on journalists' desks daily. If it isn't clear to you, it won't be to them.

Restrict your story to one A4-size page. Use your letterhead, as it contains your address and other contact details. Also include your contact name and phone number at the end of your story.

Your media release must be typed with, at least 1½ line spacing. Publisher, a Microsoft program, comes with a format specifically for media releases.

- Make your story clear and concise, using simple language. Have a short and punchy title.

- Do not exaggerate, tell it like it is. Remember this may appear in print and you have to be able to deliver.

- Pay attention to details such as dates and times.

◆ Double-check your spelling. This attention to detail is seen as basic courtesy by journalists.

Targeting your story

If your emphasis is on food, naturally food sections of newspapers or gourmet magazines are where your story is best suited. If you offer unique scenery, try the travel section of a weekend paper. If you have gardens that have won awards, then the home or gardening section could be an opportunity.

Prior to writing your release, read the sections you are targeting carefully to understand what it is in each story that captured the imagination of the editor and made it topical.

Get to know your local papers, their deadlines and the names of staff who you will be targeting. Being an active member of your community will enhance your chance of getting a media profile.

A week after posting your media kit follow it up with a phone call. Ask if the media kit has been received. If not, explain briefly what it is about and offer to send another copy. If they have seen it, ask them if they need more information and if they think the story is suitable.

Instead of a traditional media kit you may consider offering journalists and their partners a first-hand experience of your Bed & Breakfast. A free night's accommodation is a cheap price to pay for a glowing report in a popular magazine or travel section of a metropolitan newspaper. A journalist's visit will not necessarily provide you with fantastic copy or even an article, but 'freebies' or 'familiarisations' for journalists are part of the system, and word of mouth reports would always be to your advantage. For best effect, limit the period of the offer so journalists are less likely to put it away and forget about you. Good editorial coverage may not make your business, but can provide icing on the cake of your marketing plan. Well done, it is economical and effective.

Public relations are also about relations with your local community. Build up positive relationships with local clubs and business organisations, so you and your business become known and trusted by the locals. Public relations may also include sponsoring a fundraising event, horse race or local sports team for example.

There are a number of books available on how to make public relations work for you. The media unit of your state tourism association can also provide information and support. You may wish to consider using a public relations consultancy for your initial promotion.

You advise the consultant of what you have in mind and your approximate budget, they will come back to you with a proposal. The advantage of a good PR consultancy is that they already have the writing skills and media contacts to make the exercise effective, so your budget can be money well spent.

> **TIP**
> Think carefully before spending money on advertising, particularly in the choice of medium.

HOW MUCH MARKETING DO I NEED?

Any expenses incurred in promoting your business can be set against any tax you might pay on your profits, however this can be complicated when you are first embarking upon your venture.

Consult your accountant before spending any money. What you should not do is decide that you need a certain type of advertisement just because that's what everyone else does. You must decide what is appropriate to your B&B at any given time. You should, however, have some idea about who it is you are trying to attract and how best to reach them.

A marketing plan and budget needs to be developed in conjunction with your business plan.

BED & BREAKFAST GUIDES

You need to be included in a few Bed & Breakfast guides – that is a reality. When you are making your choice you should look at the following:

- ◆ How many years has the guide been in existence?
- ◆ How many copies does the publisher print?
- ◆ How many copies do they actually sell or give away?
- ◆ Where is it for sale or distributed?
- ◆ How much is it sold for, or is it free?
- ◆ How often and when does the guide come out?
- ◆ Do you like the method of presentation?
- ◆ Do they have a related web site?

How much does it cost?

There are several published Bed & Breakfast and guest house guides you could consider. The following is a list of the more popular guides and contact details and price indications.

Official Guide to Bed & Breakfast Guest Accommodation (Where to Stay), which is published by:
Alastair Sawday Publishing – Special Places to Stay

The Old Farmyard
Yanley Lane
Long Ashton
Bristol BS41 9LR

This publishing house looks for people and places that they like and that will please a range of guests. They search for special personalities, architecture, furniture, decoration, history, food, general surroundings and gardens. Each B&B (or hotel, or self-catering property) in their guidebooks is a fascinating cocktail of those things, and each Alastair Sawday write-up is a reflection of them. At the heart of their choice of B&Bs is the owner. The finest and most comfortable houses have been turned down because the owner is grumpy or aloof, or the atmosphere cold. Equally, less-than-text-book-perfect houses have been chosen – some may be slightly dusty or chaotic or crumbling – but the owners are so charming they make the place irresistible.

All applicants are subject to inspection and approval by Alastair Sawday Publishing. It is not possible to simply buy a place in these guides. We suggest you click onto www.specialplacestostay .com

The entry fee depends on the number of rooms, starting at £434 for one room to £694 for six rooms all including VAT.

Ireland *(NB this includes hotels and self-catering properties)*
Bed and Breakfast Nationwide
PO Box 2100
Clacton on Sea
Essex CO16 9BW

Their brochure is distributed worldwide and features over 700 B&Bs around Britain and Ireland. The majority are family homes with a few guest houses included in town centres. All the B&Bs are included at no extra charge on their web site www.bedandbreakfastnationwide.com which is exclusively for properties in the brochure. They have a policy whereby the listings are limited per location. For example B&Bs are usually not less than ten miles apart. They only consider extra properties if the number of prospective visitors will satisfy everybody, or hosts are offering accommodation which fits into a different category.

The publishers visit all listed properties before they are accepted for the brochure. To give you some idea of the cost of advertising, the fee for 2006 is £300 for B&Bs with three bedrooms or less (£325 for those with four or more bedrooms). This includes a £30 registration fee, which goes towards the cost of visiting you. This fee is only charged in the first year.

AA Bed & Breakfast Guide
AA Hotel Services
Fanum House (15)
Basing View
Basingstoke
Hants RG21 4EA

The AA Bed & Breakfast Guide is an established market leader, with an estimated 40,000 copies printed every year. This publication is also sold by the American Automobile Association in the USA and available in Australia – a great global presence. Entries also appear on the AA website at www.theAA.com.

Shown below is an indication of the current registration and annual fees for inspection and rating, including a listing in the AA Bed & Breakfast Guide:

Registration type	Room count	2006 fee	
		£ (ex VAT)	£ (inc VAT)
Full membership	1 to 4	205.00	240.88
All Star ratings	5 to 10	250.00	293.75
	11 plus	290.00	340.00
Associate recognition		110.00	129.25

Note: Select the fee based on the number of letting rooms in your establishment.

In the first year of being listed in a B&B guide, you will get some bookings, but remember bookshops and newsagencies are going to take all year to sell copies. In the succeeding years, your bookings from this source will increase because you will be continually placed in more homes and vehicle glove compartments. The average holidaymaker does not update their accommodation guide every year, tending to hold onto their copy for a while.

TIPS

Just because you have your B&B listed in a B&B guide does not mean you can sit back and wait for the phone to ring. There are many operators who have spent thousands on promoting their business in inappropriate journals with little success.

MARKETING PLAN

A marketing plan should outline your marketing goals for a 12-month period and how you expect to achieve them through advertising, promotion, marketing and public relations. You should include the following elements:

- tourist information centres
- direct mail campaigns (including newsletters)
- public relations (community and media activities)
- advertising
- brochure stationery
- business stationery
- group promotions
- web sites
- trade and tourism shows
- any other activity that will get your Bed & Breakfast noticed by the public.

Carefully consider any promotional or marketing schemes and opportunities offered to you by your local or regional tourism organisations. The benefits here can be considerable.

Your marketing plan will identify your target market and how you plan to reach it.

Do not forget your local community. Word of mouth is the best advertising for any business. Locals will continually be asked for their accommodation recommendations.

Join your local Chamber of Commerce, Rotary or Lions Clubs. Include membership fees, donations and sponsorships in your marketing plan budget.

Also allow for hidden costs such as photography, artwork design and production. A contingency of 12% will allow for incidentals and price rises for the year.

BROCHURES

Your top marketing priorities will be to ensure that you become involved with your tourist information centre, become part of any local tourist authority initiatives, and create an effective brochure.

To enable you to ascertain what will attract your target market, look at your competitors' brochures.

Consider what you like, the cost involved, and make it happen.

Remember that you can make a one-colour brochure be as effective as a four-colour brochure if you use the medium carefully. You must ensure your brochure is well written, easy to read, attractive and informative.

> **TIP**
>
> Don't think about putting your rates in your brochure. Print your brochure and have a computer generated insert with rates. This will ensure you can use your brochure long after your rates have gone up, i.e. its so-called shelf-life can be extended indefinitely.

NEWSLETTERS

Newsletters are a great way to communicate with your community and with past guests. Microsoft Publisher has a number of templates you can adapt for your Bed & Breakfast. These are a great way to create a positive presence in your community and reinforce all the elements of your marketing plan. These newsletters need not be expensive. You can design them on your computer, photocopy them, or email them to your mailing list.

If you include interesting topics and amusing text, they may be passed on to friends. You might want to have the occasional special offer to ascertain effectiveness.

BUSINESS STATIONERY

Your business stationery should reflect the design of your brochures and the style of your B&B itself. You need to ensure all of the aspects of promotion are part of one cohesive package.

Get a professional photographer to photograph your B&B. They may cost what is considered a lot of money, but it will be worth it and you'll have the transparencies forever. The photos of your property can be used on your web site, in brochures and your advertisements.

14

The Fundamentals of Business

No matter what the financial or personal expectations for your new venture, it is a business and you need to treat it with the gravity it deserves. You will find it impossible to achieve the results you want without a blueprint of how you plan to get there.

In this chapter we aim to give you all the advice you need to get you started in your venture.

Find the workbook we talked about in the first chapter and write down your answers to the following questions:

- Do you have any business experience? Write down how you believe you can use this experience in your new business.

- Do you have any other experiences you can draw on? How do you believe they will help you?

- Have you spoken to an accountant or financial adviser?

- Have you contacted your national tourism office or local tourism organisation to get information on your country's tourism statistics?

◆ Have you spoken to your national or regional Bed & Breakfast association? Have you contacted its national office?

◆ Have you determined the financial goals you have for the business?

◆ Have you discussed with your financial adviser the effect that turning your house into a business will have on your financial affairs?

◆ If applicable, have you registered for VAT? Talk to your financial adviser for more information.

> **TIP**
>
> Make a practical, concrete business plan, with seven parts implementation for every one part strategy.

◆ Have you looked at various tourism industry publications?

◆ Have you sought the opinions of potential customers and suppliers?

◆ Have you worked out a financial plan to supplement your income while you build your business?

FINANCING

In the first year of your new enterprise you should try to finance your venture yourself. However, if additional funding is necessary you need to contact your small business association, your bank or credit union, or a financial adviser. Remember, all start-up businesses need initial seed capital and B&B is not an exception.

CHOOSING A LEGAL STRUCTURE

Choosing the legal structure within which your business will trade is one of the first decisions you will need to make. You must discuss the best options for you with your solicitor and financial adviser.

To help you prepare for the meeting, we are providing you with a synopsis of your options. You must not make your final decision based on this, as each business's financial position is different and only your solicitor and your financial adviser have the tools to decide which structure best suits your situation.

It is worth noting at this point that you must be honest with your financial adviser and solicitor about your financial position. They will make the decisions regarding your financial affairs based on the information you give them. If you withhold information it will only be to your financial detriment.

Sole trader

The main advantage of being a sole trader is that you are your own boss. The profits are all yours, but so are the losses. You make all the decisions relating to the business yourself – something that can be both a positive and a negative. Tax breaks are usually not as generous. The main disadvantage is that you are personally liable for any business debts, which could put your personal assets at risk.

Partnership

A partnership requires two or more people. It has the advantage of pooling resources: financial, experience, brains. It also disperses the risk. Commonly cited disadvantages are disagreements over decision-making and unequal distribution of work. A partnership agreement is an essential tool that will clarify from the outset the responsibilities of each partner. The time spent working out this at the beginning of the partnership minimises possible disagreements later. Your solicitor can help you draw up this agreement.

Company

A company is a separate entity from its shareholders and as such continues to exist when members change. It is created by incorporation under the Corporations Law. The company structure allows you to separate your personal activities from your business activities. Tax advantages are good but you may still incur personal liability for the liabilities of the company.

Trusts

This is definitely a decision for your financial adviser. Trusts are administered by the trustee for the benefit of the beneficiaries of the trust. There are a few different types of trusts and your financial adviser will best be able to advise you of their benefits.

REGISTERING A BUSINESS NAME

Be sure to register your business name, for example, Mount Tavy Cottage – so you to protect your investment. What is a business name? It is a name used by any person, partnership or company and trust for carrying on a business, unless it is the same as their own name. It is advisable to consult a solicitor before using a business name. You should also check local phone books and any relevant trade journals or magazines, to see if any other business is already using the name. If it is, you could face legal difficulties. See Useful Addresses at the end of this book for contact points.

SETTING YOUR ROOM RATE

Having decided what needs to be done in getting your house ready for Bed & Breakfast, you are probably wondering, when you see that mental picture of the property already finished, what your room rate should be in the first operating year.

We suggest that you take a calculated guess. Let us assume, for the sake of this exercise, that your guess is £40/€40 per night per room. Look up a B&B guide and find two properties that already charge £40/€40 per night and book yourself in. Be sure that the two properties are located in a similar environment, but not in the same locality, as yours. For example, if your property is a coastal one then find two others that are also located on the coast.

On checking in, you only need one night in each property, tell the host that you are shortly opening a Bed & Breakfast and that you would be grateful if they could share their experiences with you. Most B&B operators are happy to oblige.

While there, take the opportunity to check the level of hosting and facilities offered for £40/€40 per night. Have a quick look in the guest book and note what comments previous guests have made. You may find that one out of every three remarks relate directly to the intrinsic beauty of the gardens. These comments may be the reason why the B&B is so popular.

After you have stayed in the two selected B&B properties, revisit your own mental picture of your finished B&B and you might find that what you are going to offer could attract a room rate of £50/€50 per night or conversely, £30/€30 per night. In this way, you are going to make a more informed decision.

Determining pricing levels and pricing policies is the major factor affecting revenue. Factors such as demand, the market price, and customer responsiveness to price changes, influence the price levels. Other factors such as a convenient location or a more personalised service may allow a Bed & Breakfast to charge a higher room rate.

TIP

Don't underestimate the cost of food when setting your room rate. If you provide a gourmet breakfast you need to make money out of it.

Under the Sleeping Accommodation Price Display Order 1997, all accommodation houses who have more than four guest rooms must display in a prominent place, the minimum and maximum room rates that have been set.

Market mix

Now we get to the fun part. Let us assume that your proposed room rate is £40/€40 per night and that you have three guest rooms, all with their own en suites, and priced the same. We assume that in the first operating year your occupancy rate is targeted at 40%. That means we have approximately 21 weeks of projected bookings, which represents 146 days × three guest rooms equals 437 room nights. If every booking was worth £40/€40 then the annual turnover would be £17,472/€17,472.

But will all of your bookings be direct? We need to now consider 'market mix', which is to suggest that your bookings may come from different sources that attract different levels of pricing. In the table shown, we list the various booking sources and the room rates they could attract.

Booking source	Room nights sold (no)	Percentage share (%)	Room rate charged (£)(€)	Receipts (£) (€)
Direct	262 bed nights	60	40	10,488
Off peak	44	10	35	1,530
Corporate	44	10	30	1,311
Internet	66	15	40	2,622
T/Operator	22	5	30	656
Total	437	100	38 = Average room rate	16,606

In this example, actual receipts show that the average room rate was £38/€38 per night not £40/€40 as first thought. This demonstrates the effect of market mix. Ideally, you do some research in order to gauge where your bookings are likely to originate and budget accordingly. If you find that the vast majority of bookings originate from sources that attract a low room rate then you may wish to adjust your marketing strategy and in turn your projected profit and loss figures. Don't forget seasonality factors.

TAXATION AND THE BED & BREAKFAST

As in most small enterprises, there is a range of business tax regulations governing the running of a Bed & Breakfast. Rules governing the business rate payments by guest accommodation establishments have been in place for some years. However, the rigorous approach in recent times taken by the valuation offices has become a significant factor in many local economies.

So what are business rates?

Business rates are a national tax on the occupation of non-domestic property paid to, and administered by, central government although the revenue is used to provide local services. With a few specific exceptions, each non-domestic property has a rateable value, which is based on the market rent it would be expected to command. A B&B property is deemed domestic and therefore subject to normal council tax in some places, rather than business rates if:

◆ you intend not to provide short stay accommodation for more than six people at any one time in the coming year, or

◆ the property is your sole residence and the Bed & Breakfast use is subsidiary to the private use.

As a rough guide, if half or more of the whole house (not just bedrooms) is devoted to B&B guests at anyone time, then the property is likely to be business rated. We suggest strongly that you consult with your accountant or tax agent as to your true position.

Capital gains tax

When you sell a property you may have to pay capital gains tax (CGT), not on the whole amount you sell it for, but on the gain you make in selling it.

However, there are various tax reliefs available. See leaflet CGT1 'Capital gains tax'.

VAT

With VAT, as applicable, there is much your business will need to do to ensure it is compliant. The other concern for you and your taxation is that you are turning, in most cases, your family home into a business. **You will need very good taxation advice prior to taking in your first guest.** Make this a top priority.

COMPUTER LITERACY

Computers have become an important factor in our daily lives. Everywhere we go there seems to be a computer involved, either when banking, visiting a doctor or dentist and at the check-out counters of any supermarket or department store.

School children are taught how to use computers as part of their education. Typewriters are now something out of a bygone era. We now depend on computers to operate a vast range of software programs that enable us to run our business more effectively.

It is important, therefore, that all of society accepts the challenge and becomes computer literate. Not to do so can restrict our contributions in the knowledge-based information era that we all now live in.

Throughout the country there are many locally based learning faculties or tertiary colleges, which run introduction or beginner computer courses at very competitive rates.

If you have not already done so you should enrol yourself in one now. The longer you leave becoming technologically literate, the more difficult it is going to be.

PURCHASING A COMPUTER
Computers have continued to become more powerful with the release of every new model. The computer you buy today may be a similar price to the one you bought a few years ago but the capability will be much greater for the same price. Greater storage capacity, faster speed and clearer graphics are some of the changes we have seen in the past few years. This all means that virtually any 'state of the art' computer you buy will be more than adequate for running standard business software. The golden rule is to work out what software you need and then buy a computer that will run the software.

If you have a requirement for graphic design or are inclined to play a game after work that calls for high-speed graphics then you might need to look at a higher-grade specification. Any reputable retailer will be able to advise you.

A standard range of software would include business/accounting software, a word processor and a spreadsheet. The software manufacturers will specify the hardware required to run their product.

The Internet
The past few years have seen the Internet move from a position of being a novelty to that of being an integral part of business. The Internet now provides us with online banking, email, telephone directory assistance, maps, music, video, and in fact information on any topic you can imagine.

Computers were connected to the telephone line using a modem but this is now rapidly being replaced by a high speed broadband connection. If you are using the Internet just for email or banking you may still be able to make do with a dial-up connection. However, the facilities available on the Internet entice us to do much more than use it at this basic level. As we use the Internet more and more the slow speed of a dial-up connection becomes a frustration and the faster broadband connections are easier to justify.

SEARCH ENGINES
Whether you believe that the Internet is of real value to those in B&Bs, or just plain old hype, there is one point upon which most of us will agree: a lot of information can be found on the Internet. We can all agree that information is a key input to any business process. In fact, it's the availability of information, not the lure of making money on the Net that should take first priority for Bed & Breakfast owners as they merge into Internet traffic.

While there are several ways to find and distribute information on the Internet, for example mailing lists and email, the most accessible is the World Wide Web. But because there is no central depository for storing, locating, and retrieving web documents, the system would be useless without the search tools that give users an opportunity of finding the information they want.

It is important for B&B operators to understand how search tools operate. A working knowledge of common search tools will help you save time, find hidden opportunities, avoid mistakes caused by lack of information, and make your Internet marketing efforts more productive.

There are several good sources of information about search tools that can be found in public libraries, and tertiary colleges, many of which run short courses on this subject. Different information sources are directed toward different types of users: researchers, library professionals, web marketers and web developers.

The focus of this information is of interest to B&B owners as you try to make the most of what the Internet has to offer.

The objective is to:

* provide general information about search tools
* provide some basic searching tips
* provide ideas for creating 'search friendly' web sites.

Search tools seem rather straightforward. You go to a search site such as Google, Yahoo! or Bullseye, type in a keyword or two and it returns descriptions of web documents that meet your search criteria. Unfortunately, like so many other aspects of the Internet, searching for information is both easy and difficult to do. There are several reasons for this:

- Different types of searches require different search tools.
- Search procedures vary among different search tools.
- Different search tools will yield different results from identical queries.
- It is often necessary to use more than one search tool to get reliable results.
- The syntax of a search may dramatically affect results.
- Simple searches will often yield thousands of documents that satisfy the search criteria.

If your intention is to develop your own a web site, then knowledge about search tools is important for other reasons. Much of the traffic to your site will come from directories and search engines. Decisions you make about content and design will affect the likelihood of potential guests visiting your site. Therefore, this is not an issue that should be left entirely up to the web designer or a submission service. You must understand how and why visitors will find your site in order to influence that process.

The term 'search engine' is often used as a catch-all phrase for search tools. It is more accurate to use 'search engine' to describe one type of search tool and 'directory' to describe the other. The confusion stems from the fact that both types enable users to search an index or database. The difference is in the way the index is created.

People who review web sites and categorise them by subject, create directory indexes. Search engines are used by specialised software tools to automatically visit sites and index their contents. Web sites are submitted to a directory for review and either included within one or more categories or rejected by the reviewer.

Because of the human element involved, directory indexes are much smaller than search engine indexes (thousands of pages versus millions of pages).

Users find information by either:

◆ moving through progressively narrower categories
◆ using the directory's 'search' capacity.

A directory search generally involves entering one or more keywords. The directory will then return a list of categories that contain relevant sites, or of individual web sites that contain one or more of the keywords, or a combination of both. The list will not necessarily be in any particular order.

Software programs called 'robots' compile search engine indexes. Generally, either the site's creator or a submission service submits web site addresses, or URLs. This prompts a robot to visit the site and index most, or all, of the site text.

Search engine users find information by performing a keyword search, but while a simple search capability is adequate for a directory, sophisticated techniques may be needed to retrieve meaningful results from a large search engine database.

Since each search engine has its own index, a given site may be indexed by some search engines and not others. Different search engines use different formulas to find web pages that match the user's query, and then rank the matching pages according to relevance. Resubmitting your web site to the numerous search engines is one way of making sure you appear early in the list of properties displayed. There are now people who specialise in providing just that service.

It is therefore possible to enter the same search criteria into two different search engines and receive two different sets of results.

CREATING A WEB PAGE

The best way to go about creating a web page is to spend time studying the web, looking at as many pages as possible and determining what works and what doesn't. Buy a WYSIWYG editor, similar to FrontPage98, as they have useful tutorials and samples.

When you see a page you like that someone else has done, save it and learn the HTML so you know how it was done. You can then adapt the same for your own requirements.

On the web there are many sites that have tutorials and explanations of every aspect of web site design and implementation. Read reviews of books on the Internet for hints and tips. Spend time on your site and experiment. Create a style. Keep it simple and start small as you can always make it striking and involved later on.

Publish and announce your site to friends, search engines and directories, but most of all refine the site and widen your goals and learning experiences. It may well be that the best option is to hook onto a community web site or source local directories to appear on. Seek local advice, as with every aspect of your B&B business.

Your web design must reflect your goals and once those needs have been identified and an agreed structure is in place, then the site design and construction can commence. This process is very different from designing a newspaper advertisement, which can remain static, as it needs to be maintained and updated at regular intervals.

Be sure that you clearly determine the goals of your Bed & Breakfast site. Is the goal to provide a service, list your property or to supply some other service such as an index or registry? Visitors to your site will be looking for the listed material:

◆ Who are the hosts?
◆ What facilities do you offer?
◆ What are your room rates?
◆ How can you be contacted?
◆ Why should I stay at your B&B instead of someone else's?
◆ Can I book directly from the site?
◆ What is the availability like on my required dates?

Make sure that your web site is easy to navigate to allow everyone to find you. Have navigation buttons or text with informative descriptions that enables the visitor to know where they are going and what to expect.

Have a contents page that lists the features of your Bed & Breakfast site, and be sure it's interesting enough to ensure a return visit. Visual aids, particularly for accommodation, are very important. Have a photographer take very good photos of your establishment.

A well-designed web site can become an effective marketing and selling tool for your Bed & Breakfast. If you don't feel up to the challenge of designing it yourself there is an abundance of web designers who will design one for you for fees ranging from the very high to the very low.

But beware, like everything else, your web site must have a professional appearance if you're not going to waste your money. Be careful whom you choose to set up your site. There are charlatans who will charge thousands for a service that shouldn't cost more than two or three hundred at the very most. Ask to see examples of their work and the 'hits' they are attracting (the number of people who look at the sites and the average time spent on it). In the future, it could well become the major instrument for generating bookings.

Again, research will pay dividends. Once your web site is up and running you will need to make sure people can find it.

CHOOSING AN INTERNET PROVIDER
When connecting to the Internet, be sure to shop around for the deal that matches your needs. Firstly, estimate the number of hours per month you are most likely to be on the Net along with the amount of download time. We suggest that you start out with a modest number of hours and download time, as you should be able to alter the terms of your arrangement with the chosen service provider.

An estimated 987 million people are connected to the Internet as calculated for the beginning of 2006 and this number is expected to increase by 8% per year to the year 2010, Currently, an estimated 47% of all UK households (26,523,430) are connected to the Internet with 56 million European households expected to be on this year. An estimated 43% of all those people who have Internet access will buy travel related products this year. Are you ready?

15

Writing Your Business Plan

WHY HAVE A BUSINESS PLAN?

In discussion with my colleague Wal Reynolds we formulated a structure for a business plan as written analysis of your business. It will look at:

- your operations
- your resources
- your markets
- your plans for the future.

While a business plan can be seen simply as a management tool to help your business survive and grow, it also provides you, as a B&B operator, with a surprising array of benefits.

It should allow you to manage your business more effectively, set your business goals, measure your performance against your targets and allow you to recognise and cope with change.

The biggest benefit to you, however, will come from the process of writing the business plan, rather than the actual written plan itself. In writing the plan, *you* have to answer three questions:

1. Where is my business right now?
2. Where do I want it to be?
3. How will I get there?

To answer these questions you need to research your business and your market, to decide what to do, how to do it, when to do it and discover the resources you will require, which, naturally, include finances. At first glance the analysis seems daunting, but this book is designed to assist you at every step to write your own plan. It will provide you with the format, the worksheets and the sources of help and information you will need.

Out of all this, the key benefits you will receive are *confidence* and *control* and *a basis for sound decision making*.

Writing your own business plan will give you confidence in your ability to effectively manage and control your B&B operation.

Once you have written a plan, it can be used to help you obtain finance and loan funds from your bank or financial institution. Your plan can also assist you in your approach to potential suppliers, potential investors in your business, or even as support documents for tender submissions and applications.

Finally, the time may come when you will want to sell your B&B, guest house or lodge. The fact that you have a current business plan will immediately enhance the sale of your business to any potential purchaser.

YOUR STARTING POINT

It is not enough to simply say, 'Yes, I'll write a business plan', and try to fit it in amongst all your other work

priorities. Writing a plan requires full commitment, and will require the allocation of resources such as time, money and staff. It may well mean that you have to find back-up for yourself while you leave your normal operational duties to research and write your plan.

Once you have set a completion date, consider promoting this date to family and colleagues; your partners, your staff and your professional team. In this way you are creating a self-discipline tool to ensure that:

◆ you actively use the planning time you have allocated yourself
◆ you stick to your deadline of producing your completed plan.

It is also important that you accept the fact that you can and should obtain help in writing your plan. Don't try to do it all yourself – use your partner, your staff and your professional support team to assist you in getting your plan on paper.

By involving your team in the creation of your plan you are also ensuring their co-operation and commitment in implementing the plan once it is written.

The next step in the preparation of your plan is to organise your approach and your information. This means you should be deciding on a format for it. There is no universal model for business plans, but you should remember that it needs a base, or foundation, which is simply an audit of where your business is – right now. This will enable you to decide where you want to go, what you want to achieve, what you have to change and what actions you should take. It will also allow you to measure the current and future costs, revenues and financial returns of your business.

The apparent complexity of this task is perhaps the main reason why most B&B owners avoid writing their own business plan. However, the process is surprisingly simple if you divide your plan into components, such as:

- index
- executive summary
- mission statement
- current status
- objectives, strategies and milestones
- forecasts
- appendices.

The following sections will look at each of these components in turn. Worksheets, which have been designed to help you create your own plan, are included.

Your business plan should be a fluid working document and an evolving process. You can gather information on more than one section at a time, and data gathered in the later stages may alter your thinking and any conclusions developed during your earlier work.

Remember that it is important to keep written notes on all key points and arguments to provide an effective audit trail for your assumptions.

THE BUSINESS PLAN STRUCTURE

The index
This section is the organiser for your plan and it should contain the standard information that is normal in any business plan.

Title sheet
The title page is your cover sheet and is preferably shown on your letterhead, with a standout centered heading, e.g.

BUSINESS PLAN
FOR
BED & BREAKFAST BUSINESS NAME – 200X TO 200Y

It is strongly advised that a confidentiality notice be displayed at the bottom of this page.

The list of contents
This page is a road map for your plan. It is designed to tell the reader what is included in your plan and where to find it. It is traditionally the first page following the title page. When you start to write your plan, create a draft version of the contents page to help you organise your approach. As your planning evolves, so too will your contents page.

The following pro-forma shows sections your own business plan should contain.

Contents	Page number
Title page	
List of contents	
Contact information	
Professional support	

Executive summary

Mission statement

Current situation
   Business overview
   Vision statement
   Organisational structure
   Market outline
   Competition
   SWOT analysis

Objectives, strategies and milestones
   Key objectives
   Strategies for success
   Milestones

Forecasts and reports
   Sales
   Income and expenditure
   Cash flow
   Balance sheet

Appendices

Contact information
This is simply gives the details of the people who may be

contacted for further information on the plan or the business. Don't forget to include the email address where appropriate.

Professional support

All that is required in this section is a single page that outlines the names and contact details of your professional advisers. These advisers should include:

◆ your accountant
◆ your solicitor
◆ your banker
◆ your business adviser/mentor
◆ your B&B association or tourist association
◆ your insurer.

The executive summary

This one-page summary is the key to your plan. Unless you get it right, your target readers will not want to proceed any further.

TIP
Don't try to write your plan without asking your professionals for help.

> The summary is your plan in miniature.

Its contents depend upon the goal of your plan, i.e. to attract potential investment, to support a loan facility or maybe it is simply the internal control you want for your operation, or perhaps support for a tender proposal you are submitting.

Your first paragraph should contain the name of your B&B, together with its location. The paragraph should continue to define clearly the nature and purpose of your plan, stating exactly what you want to do and what precisely you need. Then, we suggest that you continue your executive summary with a brief (but general) outline of who you are, your management team and their skills and a summary of the market you are serving. Briefly mention what makes you special or unique, that is, your distinctive competence, which is the recognition of a particular skill, resource or asset of your organisation. It is the factor that makes you stand out from your competition. Then, outline your main objectives and your strategies for success.

Finally, include your projections of sales (bed nights and revenue), profitability estimates and other key financial information.

> **TIP**
> Nobody needs a long-winded business plan. Today, no one is interested in a business plan more than 30 pages long.

You should write the executive summary in draft form before you start to write your plan. This will give you a focus. Write your plan, and then, when it is written, go back and amend your draft summary.

The current situation

The purpose of this section is to establish a planning base and to provide the readers with an understanding of your business.

It should start with an overview of your business then expand to outline your staff and organisation, and then proceed to examine the market in which you operate.

The business overview

Also known as your business profile, your business overview is a short (one page) snapshot of your business. The first paragraph should provide key essential information such as the business name of your establishment, trading names, your location, legal structure, taxation numbers, web site address (if applicable), and membership of any B&B or tourism authority.

The next paragraph should expand to give the reader a quick insight into your actual operations, i.e. style of building, lettable rooms, main facilities, industry rating, seasonality etc. Given this outline, you should then talk about your trading history, highlighting key achievements and developments. It is at this stage that you spell out your distinctive competence – i.e. what skills, abilities, strengths or assets you have that your competition lacks.

In other words – what makes you different?

Many business plan writers find the ideal way to conclude their business overview is by formally writing their mission statement and presenting it before or after the executive summary.

To develop a mission statement, look firstly at your vision and ask, 'How would I like my business to be seen and remembered?' This mission is simply a broad, philosophical explanation of your business. A typical example of a mission statement for your Bed & Breakfast could be:

'We provide an ambient, romantic experience
for dreamers everywhere.'

Vision statement
To put your mission into practice, you should develop a vision

statement which is a brief, realistic and achievable outline of what you have to do to achieve your goals, i.e. your mission. This can go at the end of your business overview.

The vision statement is also a concise way of defining exactly the business that you are in. Focus on your customer needs and the benefits you can, or should, provide. If you do this you will realise that you are in the business of hosting guests, not in the business of Bed & Breakfasts.

Your vision statement should be no more than two sentences, and it should explain:

◆ why your business exists
◆ what it does
◆ what it hopes to achieve.

As an example, consider the following:

Vision statement

'The Lakeside Retreat' is the ideal romantic destination for honeymoon couples and anniversary celebrations. In providing an unparalleled service for our guests, we will maintain our ranking in the nation's list of the Top 20 most romantic venues.

Once you have provided the reader with an overview of your business, the next step is to look at the elements of that business.

You and your team, and your administration

Any business is only as good as its people, and this is particularly so in a service business such as a Bed & Breakfast, guest house or lodge.

There is no set format for writing this section, as each business is unique. Many B&Bs are just one or two person operations. In these cases this section would contain a short explanation of this fact and show:

1. A profile of the owner(s). This outline should highlight the skills and experience that the owners are bringing into the business, together with any other qualifications and relevant achievements.

2. Back-up arrangements such as locums or casual staff and/or family who can be put into place if the principals were absent or incapacitated.

In larger establishments, this section should still contain profiles of the principals and key staff where appropriate. It should be backed up by:

◆ An organisation chart showing lines of authority and responsibility.
◆ A list of employees containing names, classifications and rates of pay.

A weekly roster will ensure that all areas are able to be serviced. This roster should contain the names and contact details of back up staff who could be called upon as required.

More detailed information, such as emergency contact details, employee records and position descriptions should not be included, but they should exist in your confidential filing system.

While it is critical to have good people to run your B&B, it is also vital to have effective administration. Comment should also be made in this section of your procedures for handling and converting enquiries, the registration and billing systems and programs, record keeping (including taxation), and cash handling procedures.

Your market outline

Your existing market

This section is designed to provide an overview of the market in which you operate. Perhaps the easiest way to write this section is in two stages, firstly as a broad outline, then as a detailed analysis of your performance, and that of your competition. Where is it? How big is it? Is it growing or declining? Who are your competitors? When are your high and low periods? What type of guests does your business service and where do they come from?

You should also highlight any key factors that you believe, have or will, affect your market e.g. legislation, larger community events, e.g. Olympic Games, or socio-economic factors such as airline collapses or natural disasters.

Remember that this is a summary only in general terms, but you may care to support it with a map showing your location and that of your competitors, and key attractions and features. Industry performance can also be supported by graphs of visitor numbers, total sales, etc.

To get this information you will need to analyse your own records as well as conducting market research from industry and association reports, the Internet, government departments, directories, and so on. Remember, however, that your outline presents a general picture. It is important not to confuse the picture with too many details, or too many words.

Your current market position
Once you have an overall picture of your existing market, you should be looking at examining, in detail, your current market situation. What has been your trading history and what are you selling, to whom, and why?

In writing this section it is perhaps timely to remind yourself of a few basic but pertinent facts:

♦ Your guests are customers – they are the source of your income.
♦ Not everyone wants to stay at your B&B or guest house.
♦ You have competitors who are trying, non-stop, to take your clients from you.
♦ There is no client loyalty – they will only come back as long as you are giving them what they want.
♦ Discount levels must be balanced – protect your bottom-line. There is no such thing as a 'profitable loss'.
♦ The percentage of repeat business will have a bearing on how you allocate expenditure, for example, advertising.
♦ The average pound or euro spent per person is another important consideration.

The first information you should be extracting from your records is a trading history. What were your sales, by month, over say the last 12 months? Or over two years? See if you can provide a trend of your trading activity that you can use as a base to estimate future income. You may have the information readily available from your computer.

Develop a worksheet that allows you to identify any factors that may have affected your occupancy and income, e.g. local shows, adverse weather, special television promotions, etc. The worksheet should also allow you to dissect your income into key source areas – e.g. room hire, restaurant, sales of gift lines, commissions, equipment hire, etc. These avenues of income are often neglected or overlooked by B&B operators.

Once you have established a trading history the next questions refer to your market groups or segments:

1. What type of clients do you attract? If you were to analyse them, could they be grouped as:
    – corporate clients
    – more affluent guests
    – middle-income couples/singles
    – short-break holiday market
    – families
    – budget market
    – gay/lesbian
    – overseas visitors
    – groups?

2. Further dissection could also be considered, for example,
    – the short-break market categories
    – romantic holidays
    – celebrating special occasions

– visiting friends and relatives

– fishing trips etc.

Don't just assume that you know the answers. Ask the question – 'Why did they stay with you?' Check your records, especially your visitor book to make sure you know the real story.

Competition
Once you have this information, you can then establish what your competition is doing – what type of clients they are attracting and why they stayed with them rather than with you. You are then in a position to move to the next stage of your planning, i.e. the construction of a SWOT analysis.

SWOT analysis
SWOT is simply a shorthand description of the **S**trengths, and **W**eaknesses of your own business, and the **O**pportunities and **T**hreats it is facing in the marketplace.

Your SWOT analysis is a two-stage exercise. In stage one, you look at your business and ask, 'How do my clients (actual and potential) see my business in relation to my competition?' plus 'What is important to them and why?' and 'What are the main points on which they will focus?'

Make a list of these key points and then analyse each one to decide if your clients would see each individual point as either:

◆ a strength that your business has and your competition does not

◆ a weakness that needs to be addressed.

Typical key points you might consider are:

Reputation	value for money, repeat clients, outstanding meals
Rating	by tourism authority or Bed & Breakfast association
Managers and staff	friendly, efficient, experienced, trained, client focused, receptive
Location	proximity to attractions, isolated, easily found, views
Facilities	secure parking, dining room, restaurant, grounds, pools, equipment, e-commerce
Décor and rooms	style, room size, presentation, themes
Promotion	coverage, effectiveness, web site, association membership, signage
Price	relative to target market
Profitability	good or bad, high or low
Rooms	size, maintenance, inclusions, access
Meals	quality, quantity, uniqueness, flexibility, use of local produce.

Involve your staff in creating this list and don't exclude any points simply because 'everyone knows that!' What is obvious to you could turn out to be a critical factor that none of your competitors have discovered.

Once you have completed your list of strengths and weaknesses, create two short lists of six key strengths and six key weaknesses, ranked in order of importance.

In stage two of your SWOT analysis, you should look at your business again, but with a different focus. Instead of looking at the *internal* factors of your business over which you have control, look this time at the industry and identify *external* factors that will affect or influence your future operations. As you identify each factor, ask 'What's in it for me?' and decide whether these factors provide you with either an opportunity for growth and profitability, or a threat to your existence or profitability.

When constructing your worksheet, stand back and think 'outside the box'. Look for changes in the marketplace, e.g. in regulations, in competitors and their activities, in economic development, technology, etc. Be aware of emerging trends in the B&B industry overseas and try to forecast the possible impact on your market.

Some examples of key points are:

Competition	development activity, closures, new competition, change of ownership, upgrades
Legislation	new requirements for B&Bs, occupational health and safety changes, award rate increases, taxation changes, insurance
Technology	e-commerce, reservation and billing software
Economic factors	recession, industry moves, industrial disputes, changes in demand

Industry promotions new tourism bodies and regional promotions

Other local news (good/bad), local and special events, e.g. conferences.

Again, involve your staff in creating and analysing these points and create a short list of opportunities and threats to focus your thinking and planning. From this SWOT analysis you have identified:

- your key strengths – which you want to protect and promote
- your key weaknesses – which you want to address and fix
- your opportunities in the marketplace – which you would like to exploit
- the potential and actual threats – to the profitability and survival of your business which must be addressed.

The issues identified in the SWOT analysis should be addressed and incorporated in your business plan. You should now know where you are. The next stage in the planning process is to look at the future and decide:

- where you want to be (your objectives)
- how to get there (your strategies)
- proof of your progress (your milestones).

TIP

If you are always putting out fires then build a sprinkler system. You can lose the forest by paying too much attention to the trees.

Some people actually do make money in spite of themselves, but most successful people plan for success.

> Start your planning process by defining exactly
> what you want – set your objectives.

Objectives, strategies and milestones

Key objectives

Objectives are concise and measurable statements, which outline
what you want to achieve within a given time span. The direction
and focus of your business objectives will come from key areas,
namely:

◆ your mission statement
◆ your personal objectives
◆ your current position analysis
◆ your SWOT analysis.

As we stated earlier, your mission statement encapsulates your
philosophy.

Your personal objectives should be explained in your vision
statement; why your business exists, what it does and what it
hopes to achieve. It is the final point – what it hopes to achieve,
that is critical in setting your objectives. In the example we gave,
the emphasis was on the desire 'To maintain our ranking in the
nation's list of Top 20 most romantic venues'. This statement sets
the focus on the style and theme of operation and the type of
guests to be targeted, the promotion to be undertaken and the
quality of the accommodation and surroundings that must be
maintained.

> As an owner of a business, it is important to remember that *your* business is only a means of achieving what you *want* in your private life.

In simple terms your private life must take precedence over your business life – even though in practice, the reverse seems to happen more often than not. Your personal objectives could well impact on your business objectives by limiting your business hours, influencing your investment decisions, balancing family and guests' usage of your facilities, etc.

Your current position analysis will give you a base for setting your business objectives, and your SWOT analysis will give you focus.

The mechanics of setting objectives are not difficult. Instead of thinking of your business as a whole, try breaking it down (in your mind) into a few key areas. Pick a date in the future, say six months, 12 months or even three years ahead and visualise how you perceive that key area at that time.

To work though an example, start by selecting your key areas, say:

Your operation
◆ facilities, systems
◆ management and staff
◆ marketing – clients
◆ promotions, offers, services
◆ finance and funding results, e.g. profitability, return on investment, occupancy
◆ industry ratings, etc.

Then (after consulting your vision statement, your current situation analysis and the key points in your SWOT analysis) write down what you want to achieve. Examples could be:

By . . / . . / . . . .
- To have new computerised booking and billing systems.
- To increase total occupancy by x%.
- To upgrade our industry rating to say four stars.
- To conduct a six week study tour of B&Bs in the European community.
- To increase gross takings to an annual level of . . . . .
- To lift net profit from the existing x% to y%.
- To establish a corporate clientele of at least 50% of total monthly sales.

While it is vital that you include a completion date in your objectives, remember that you don't have to achieve all your results immediately. Some objectives will require a longer time frame. Your worksheet should make provision for current, medium- and long-term objectives, (short-term: six months time period, medium-term: six to two years and long-term objectives: two to five years).

Also, don't try to be too ambitious. Pick out the objectives you consider to be most critical to your operation – say three to four objectives from each key area, e.g. operational, staff, marketing and financial.

> The next step is to make your objectives happen
> by developing your strategic plans.

Strategies for success
A **strategy**, in lay terms, is simply a planned course of action designed to achieve a given objective. The easiest way to develop a strategy is to look at your objective, ask the basic question, 'How are we going to do that?' and start brainstorming.

Involve your partner/s and your team and don't dismiss any ideas in the initial stage as 'no use', or 'too hard' or 'can't be done'. It is often the 'way-out' or 'stupid' ideas that breed genius and results.

Once you have all the ideas on paper, then analyse them and come up with a summary of your proposed course of action. As an example, let us assume that your analysis of your current position has shown your major client segment to be from the budget market, and despite the high quality of your offerings, you are catering for few of the more affluent guests. Furthermore, despite your proximity to the central business district (CBD) you have no corporate clientele. Just to make the situation worse, your SWOT analysis also reveals that the three nearby hotels are displaying 'no vacancy' signs on a continuous basis.

On the strength of this information, you and your team can see an opening in the corporate market, which can command a better room rate, midweek occupancy and a different type of guest. You and your team develop an objective – 'To develop a corporate clientele of at least 50% of our average monthly bookings within the next 12 months'.

To achieve this objective, the strategies you develop could be summarised along the lines of: 'To establish the accommodation needs and preferences of corporate clients and use the results of this research to change our image, our offerings and our promotional activities and effectiveness'.

From this strategy statement it is obvious that much has to be done before the objective can be achieved. A list of jobs, or action steps, should be created and responsibility should be allocated for their completion. In creating this list, allocate completion times to each action step and also try to estimate the cost of each step.

Such a list could look like the example on page 280.

As you can see, this example is not exhaustive – but it goes a long way towards organising a plan of action to achieve the objective of attracting corporate clients. It is all very well to have such a plan, but what can you do to make it work?

Milestones
Milestones, as the name implies, are physical guides to advise you of your location and progress along your journey. In the implementation of your business plan, milestones serve the same purpose, i.e. to advise you of your progress with your action steps.

The milestones for the action steps in our example could be simply:

- client list created
- customer survey completed
- analysis mechanism established

Action step	Reponsibility	Due date	Cost £€
Research			
List of potential corporate clients	SW	18/7/..	NA
Needs audit of clients	SW	18/7/..	NA
Establish origin of clients	SW	18/7/..	NA
Conduct own promotional audit	SH		NA
Create a business event diary for next 12 months	SH	18/7/..	NA
Promotion			
Design and develop new publicity folder	ADS	20/8/..	1,500
Print and distribute new folders	ADS	27/8/..	2,500
Inclusion in community web site	RDA	20/8/..	400
Implement changes suggested from own promotional audit	ADS	Set program	TBA
Premises upgrade			
Provide work centres in each room	CD	1 month	800 each
Install ADSN facility	CD	24/7/..	500, + 130/mth
Selling activity			
Join Chamber of Commerce	SW	Now	250
Join Rotary Club	SW	Now	300
Visit ten potential clients per week	All	Ongoing	NA
Place follow-up call with all guests within two weeks to obtain feedback and solicit referrals	JA	Ongoing	NA
Attend all major events on business calendar	All	Ongoing	TBA
Price policy			
Decide on new policy and discount offers where applicable	All	Now	NA
Staff			
Create new roster to service new client needs	BA	13/9/..	NIL
Reports			
Generate monthly reports on corporate clients average billing. Repeat clients, etc	SW	Monthly	NIL

- business diary created
- promotional brochure printed
- web site complete
- connection of high speed data access for PC
- others.

Create a worksheet to assist you to achieve each of your objectives by:

1. Stating your objective in writing.
2. Summarising your strategies.
3. Listing your action steps.
4. Identifying each milestone required.

Because each strategy can have a large number of action steps, your worksheet should be presented in two pages to accommodate the listing of all steps and milestones.

Forecasts and reports

Predicting the future is not an accurate science; rather it comes down to having the best guess of what you expect to happen, based on your current information. The reliability of your forecasts will depend upon your understanding of several factors, namely:

- Your base data and its quality.
- The factors you expect will influence your base data.
- Your ability to read these factors effectively.

To relate this to your own B&B operation, the base data we are talking about is from your own records, especially your sales income and operating costs. This base data provides the foundation for establishing reports used for analysis, reporting of your profitability or otherwise, taxable income, your ownership (assets and equity) and debts and liabilities.

Once you have the base data, you can identify the key factors, which you expect will influence the future performance of your operation. Examples of such factors could be:

- Weekly, monthly and seasonal trading patterns.
- Changes in your establishment, i.e. additional rooms or offerings, management approach or staff.
- The weather.
- Special events, e.g. gatherings, exhibitions.
- Changes in your image and ratings.
- Promotional activity.
- Sensitivity to price changes.
- Changes in demand, i.e. type of client, average holiday duration, competitor activity.
- Economic conditions, i.e. local, national and international.

> **TIP**
>
> A good business plan is a practical one. It must have realistic goals that can be implemented. It will guide decisions

The next step in forecasting is to consider the type of factors listed above and make value judgements about which of these factors will affect your future operations. Your SWOT analysis should have already highlighted many of these factors. Furthermore, your SWOT worksheet should have identified the main factors in order of importance.

Now comes decision time! In what way do you anticipate these factors will affect your operation and by how much?

> In simple terms, you must define your assumptions for the future operation of your business

Don't forget to ask for help in this exercise. Involve your partner(s) and your team and use professional support as a sounding board and also for specialised professional input. The final decision is yours, however – as it is your business.

Let's see how it all comes together in practice. The key forecasts you should be looking for are sales, profitability and cash.

Sales forecasts
Earlier on we talked about your trading history and suggested you use a worksheet to provide information on your sales to use as a forecasting base.

Ask the question, 'What changes to this sales history do I expect in the next twelve months?' If the answer is nil, you already have your sales forecast.

This, however, will probably not be your answer, as you should have set some objectives to reflect a change in sales history based upon your SWOT analysis and strategies.

To build up your sales forecast, start with last year's figures as a base and simply add to or subtract from these figures any changes you expect. For example:

- Increased occupancy over the Easter period (let us say, 15%) – was in April last year, but will be in March this year.

- A price rise of, say, 10% to commence in November.

- Your promotion for corporate clients should provide an additional . . . bed nights per week (Monday to Thursday) from September onwards.

- You will be offering picnic lunches from March and anticipate an acceptance rate of say ten lunches per week at . . . per time.

All this information can be easily assembled, by constructing a simple spreadsheet as shown below.

Forecasting worksheet

Activity sales period ending .../.../...

Item	Jul	Aug	Sep	Oct	Nov	Dec	Total
Previous year							
Summer boost							
Price increase				+ 10%	+ 10%	+ 10%	
Corporate clients				+ y	+ y	+ y	
Picnic lunches				+ x	+ x	+ x	
Total							

Once you have this sales forecast you can use the information to assist you in your financial planning, starting with profit and loss.

Income and expenditure

Profit and loss

The formula used to measure the profitability or otherwise of your B&B operation is:

> Sales income − direct costs = gross profit.
> Gross profit − operating costs = net
> profit (before tax and owner's drawings).

We have discussed sales income previously.

Direct costs are the actual costs you incur in the direct production of the service you provide, i.e. the food and provisions you use. They do not include all your operating expenses, which have to be paid from your margin or gross profit. Our experience in the B&B industry is that direct costs should be no more than 25% of revenue, allowing a healthy margin to cover all the other expenses.

In the past most B&B operators relied on their accountants to produce profit and loss reports for them. Today, most B&B operators are using computerised accounting systems that facilitate easy and quick access to profit and loss reports, which makes financial control and analysis of your operation so much easier. You should still involve your accountant however, in checking your computerised results and advising you of the ramifications of your profit and loss reports.

Once you have a current profit and loss report on your operation it is easy to project your future profitability. Earlier on we looked at the techniques of forecasting your sales month by month. It is just as easy to apply the same forecasting principles to forecasting your expenses and therefore your profitability.

The following table illustrates the areas to be considered when projecting your profit and loss.

Forecast profit for period ending ../../..

Item	Jul	Aug	Sep	Total
Sales income				
Cost of goods sold				
Gross profit				
Less				
Accountancy				
Advertising				
Association fees				
Bank charges				
Cleaning				
Commissions paid				
Ground upkeep				
Insurance				
Internet payments				
Laundry				
Postage and printing				
Power				
Repairs and maintenance				
Telephone				
Training				
Travelling				
Vehicle costs				
Wages and salaries				
Sundry				
Total operating costs				
Net profit				
Drawings				

Note: depreciation estimates are not included.

All your expenses are shown on one-line totals in this report. For example, if you want to look at advertising, use a worksheet to estimate the expenditure you expect to incur and the month you will have to pay for it. By spelling out when you expect to pay, it is easier to estimate cash flow – but more on that later.

Forecasting worksheet – advertising

Item	Jul	Aug	Sept	Total
Newspaper				
Association magazine				
Yellow Pages				
Folders				
Business cards				
Internet advertising				
Car signs				
B&B signage				
Giveaways				
Other				
Total advertising				

This same worksheet can also be used to summarise all your other expense areas into one-line summaries for your profit and loss reporting. Whilst your computerised accounting system can provide all this information readily, one of the advantages of doing the exercise manually is to get a 'hands-on' feel for your business. Also, while you are forecasting your expenses, make sure you keep copies of your assumptions, and even your working papers. This will enable you to back check your estimates and also to upgrade your estimates as required.

Cash flow

While your budgeted profit and loss report allows you to predict the profitability or otherwise of your operation, cash flow looks at your ability to pay your bills. Your cash flow projections will show:

◆ your income and when you expect to receive it
◆ your expenditure and when you expect to pay
◆ your projected bank balance.

In simple terms, your cash flow is constructed along the following lines:

Item	Month 1	Month 2	Month 3
Opening bank balance	x	X1	X2
+ Income			
– Expenditure			
Closing bank balance	X1	X2	X3

Your closing bank balance must equal your opening bank balance at the start of the next month.

Therefore to create your cash flow projections:

◆ establish your actual bank balance
◆ record all monthly income as you expect to receive it (refer to your sales forecasts)
◆ record all monthly expenditure summaries as you expect to pay them.

While much of this information will come from your budgeted profit and loss report, you are looking at cash flow, and will therefore have to include all cash movements, for example:

◆ other non-trading income, e.g. sale of assets, other income, etc
◆ direct production costs (cost of producing sales)
◆ purchase of assets
◆ loan repayments

◆ owner's drawings

◆ taxation payments, etc.

In your cash flow projections, remember that each entry is a one-line summary, and we have shown you how to use the forecasting worksheets to arrive at these one-line summaries. Your cash flow projection could look like this:

Item	Month 1	Month 2	Month 3	Month 12
Income				
Sales				
Other				
Total Income				
Expenditure				
Purchases				
Direct costs				
Running costs				
Drawings				
Loan repayments				
Asset purchases				
Taxation				
Other				
Total expenditure				
Opening bank balance				
Plus total income				
Less total expenditure				
Closing bank balance				

In the preparation of your business plan, your cash flow projection plays a major role as it ties everything together financially. The resultant income and expenditure from your existing operations, plus from the strategies you employ to achieve your objectives can be viewed together for the first time in your cash flow. This information allows you to play 'what if?'

scenarios if you want to see the implications of clarifying your strategies, time frames, assumptions, or whatever. It also allows you to see if you can pay your bills when they fall due or whether you should consider deferring expenditure until the funds you require are available.

The cash flow projection will also assist you to see the need for additional funds or perhaps reorganising your finances. Should you need to borrow, any potential lender will want to see:

1. A business plan – to understand your business and why you want the funding.

2. Cash flow projections – to establish your ability to repay the loan you are seeking.

3. Profit and loss statements – to establish your ability to earn a profit and thereby stay in business.

4. A balance sheet – which shows your equity in the business, and the assets you have that can act as security for any loan.

Balance sheet

A balance sheet is a financial report designed to show what a business owns and what it owes. Your balance sheet will show a list and value of current assets, e.g. cash, debtors, stock (which your business intends to convert into cash within 12 months), etc. It will also show a list and value of other assets, e.g. plant and equipment, land and buildings, vehicles and goodwill (which is an intangible asset).

On the other side, your balance sheet will list and value all liabilities the business has to repay, e.g. to lenders, suppliers, and to you (as the owner of the business). It will traditionally show debts to others as current liabilities (e.g. bank overdraft, short-term loans, creditors, etc. that have to be repaid within 12 months) and long-term liabilities which include all the long-term loans, mortgages, etc. that the business has to pay back.

Finally, it will show your equity (or proprietorship) in the business, i.e. your investment plus any profits you have retained in the business.

To summarise, a balance sheet is traditionally presented as:

Assets		**Liabilities**	
Current	_____	Current	_____
Long term	_____	Long term	_____
Intangible	_____	Total liabilities	_____
		Equity	_____
		Total liabilities	
Total assets	_____	and equity	_____

Total assets must always equal total liabilities plus equity. In looking at your balance sheet, you and any potential lender, partner or purchasers can see very quickly such things as:

◆ Your shareholding in the business and its relative size.

◆ The value of your business (current assets minus current liabilities) in the event of a forced sale of your business.

◆ Your borrowing ability, i.e. do your assets exceed your liabilities or otherwise?

◆ Your financial management (e.g. debtors *v* creditors), the size of your overdraft, and much more.

In summary, it is the financial reporting section of your plan that ties your whole business plan together. Your planning base is contained in the profit and loss statements and balance sheet of previous years. Your forecasting of the effects of your strategies will be displayed in your projected reports in which you and others will be able to see:

1. The future profitability of your business (profit and loss).
2. The ability of your business to pay its bills (cash flow).
3. What your business owns and what it owes (balance sheet).
4. Your equity in the business (balance sheet).

It is only when you put these reports together that you can see whether or not your plan can and will achieve your objectives.

Having reached this stage, you should now go back and complete your executive summary.

Appendices

The appendix section of your plan is simply a section designed to accommodate detailed working papers and other support information. It allows you to present your plan in a professional manner and avoid the trap of 'losing the plot', with too much detail in the main body of the plan. Should the reader of your plan wish to have more detail they can readily go to the appendix section. Furthermore, when you want to upgrade your business plan in the future, your working papers are easily located.

Typical support information that readers would expect to see in the appendix section are:

◆ Previous audited financial reports, e.g. profit and loss statements and balance sheets.

◆ Industry, marketing and other reports and articles referred to in the plan.

◆ Competitor publications and information, e.g. brochures, publications, etc.

◆ All other information vital to the understanding of the plan by the reader.

The appendix section should also have, as its first page, an index or contents page, for obvious reasons.

SUMMARY

We began this section by stating that a business plan is a structured analysis of your business, in writing, that looks at:

◆ your operations
◆ your resources
◆ your markets
◆ your plans for the future.

We have provided a suggested structure for your plan along with suggestions and examples to assist you as you work through and plan your own business. The real benefit to having the plan is, not surprisingly, the finished business plan, but the knowledge and control that you obtain as you analyse your operations and your market and set strategies and controls for your future performance.

This section includes extracts from the title *A Business Plan for B&B Owners* by Stewart Whyte with Wal Reynolds. The entire book can be purchased in a down-loadable, interactive format that enables you to create your own business plan. To obtain a download go to www.bnb-central.com – click British Flag then Order Publications.

Glossary

Account balance – The difference between the total debits and total credits of an account.

A la carte – Where the guest can order anything on a vast menu and only pays for what she/he eats.

Artwork – This is the name given to original material, photographs, illustrations, typesetting (lettering) etc, when making up the overall design of a printing job.

Assets – Things of value owned by a person or business.

Bad debt – A loss caused by the failure of a customer to pay what is owed.

Balance sheet – A statement at a certain date, setting out the assets, liabilities and proprietorship of a business.

Bookkeeping – The systematic recording of financial transactions in a journal, then a ledger, then a trial balance.

Camera ready artwork – Artwork prepared to a stage from which a printing plate can be made without further changes.

Capital – The wealth, including money and property used in the business.

Commission – The percentage of sale paid as a fee to an agent selling your accommodation.

Cost of goods sold – The cost of producing, converting or acquiring goods sold during a period.

Cover – Place or setting at a table. Term used by waiting staff.

Creditor – Person to whom money is owed by your business.

Debtor – Person who owes money to your business.

Email – *See Internet.*

Expenditure – Costs and charges of operating a business which decrease profits.

Franchise – A contract under which a party is licensed by another to use a name, product, service or business system, in return for a fee.

Goodwill – An intangible asset which includes business reputation, an established trading level, favourable location, licensing or exclusive trading rights.

HTML – Hyper Text Mark-up Language.

Inbound tourism – Travellers who are coming to your country from overseas.

Industrial award – Terms and conditions of employment negotiated and agreed on by employers, government and union representatives.

Internet – International computer network using phone lines (accessed by a box called modem). The Internet includes a personal message service (email).

Invoice – Document showing details of the charges for goods sold or service provided on account.

Invoicing period – A regular time period after which invoices are issued for all sales made or services provided during that period. Normally seven or 30 days.

Journal – A book of first entry in which financial transactions are entered as they occur.

Ledger – A book in which financial transactions are classified in various accounts.

Liabilities – Amounts owed by a person or business, including loans and outstanding debts.

Outbound tourism – Travellers who reside in your country and are leaving for overseas for their holiday.

Owners equity – The value of the person after liabilities have been deducted from assets. This is the amount of money that would be distributed to the owners if the business entity was dissolved.

Rack rate – The price at which you advertise your Bed & Breakfast.

Revenue – Income from business transactions.

Table d'hôte – Refers to a set menu at a set price.

Trading hours – Open for business.

Trading terms – The terms of business applied to creditors, e.g. invoices due for payment within seven days of issue.

Working capital – The capital or assets required to fund the daily operation of the business on a short-term basis. It is calculated by deducting current liabilities from current assets.

WWW – World Wide Web. The user's name for the Internet. WWW is included in all addresses (like phone numbers and extensions) on the Internet.

Useful Addresses

ENGLAND
VisitBritain UK office
Thames Tower
Blacks Road
London W6 9EL
Tel: (020) 8846 9000
Fax: (020) 8563 0302

Regional tourist boards

North England
Cheshire & Warrington Tourism Board – consumer site
www.visitchester.com

Cheshire & Warrington Tourism Board – industry site
www.cwtb.co.uk Tel: (01244) 346543

Cumbria Tourist Board – business to business site
www.cumbriatourism.info/ Tel: (01539) 444444

Cumbria Tourist Board – consumer site
www.golakes.co.uk

Lancashire & Blackpool Tourist Board – consumer site
www.visitlancashire.com Tel: (01257) 226600

Marketing Manchester – consumer site
www.visitmanchester.com

Marketing Manchester – business to business site
www.marketingmanchester.com Tel: (0161) 237 1010

The Mersey Partnership – consumer site
www.visitliverpool.com

The Mersey Partnership – business to business site
www.merseyside.org.uk Tel: (0151) 227 2727

Northumbria Tourist Board – business to business site
www.tourismnortheast.co.uk/

Northumbria Tourist Board – consumer site
www.visitnorthumbria.com

North West Tourist Board – business to business site
www.nwtourism.net

Yorkshire Tourist Board – business to business site
www.yorkshiretouristboard.net

Yorkshire Tourist Board – consumer site
www.yorkshirevisitor.com

South England
East of England Tourist Board – business to business site
www.eetb.org.uk/

East of England Tourist Board – consumer site
www.visiteastofengland.com/

Heart of England Tourist Board – business to business site
www.hetb.co.uk

Heart of England Tourist Board – consumer site
www.visitheartofengland.com

South West Tourism – business to business site
www.swtourism.co.uk/

South West Tourism – consumer site
www.visitsouthwest.co.uk

Tourism South East – consumer site
www.southerntb.co.uk

Tourism South East – consumer site
www.southeastengland.uk.com/

Visit London – consumer site
www.visitlondon.com

Visit London – corporate site
www.visitlondon.com/corporate

SCOTLAND
Aberdeen and Grampian Tourist Board – consumer site
www.agtb.org/

Angus & Dundee Tourist Board – consumer site
www.angusanddundee.co.uk/

Angus & Dundee Tourist Board – business to business site
www.angusanddundeeexchange.net/

Argyll, The Isles, Loch Lomond, Stirling – consumer site
www.scottish.heartlands.org/

Ayrshire and Arran Tourist Board – consumer site
www.ayrshire-arran.com/

Dumfries and Galloway Tourist Board – consumer site
www.galloway.co.uk/

Dundee and Angus Tourist Board – consumer site
www.angusanddundee.co.uk/

Edinburgh and Lothians Tourist Board – consumer site
www.edinburgh.org/

Greater Glasgow and Clyde Valley Tourist Board – consumer site
www.seeglasgow.com/

Highlands of Scotland Tourist Board – consumer site
www.visithighlands.com/

Kingdom of Fife Tourist Board – consumer site
www.standrews.com/fife/

Orkney Tourist Board – business to business site
www.orkneyexchange.net/

Orkney Tourist Board – consumer site
www.visitorkney.com/

Perthshire Tourist Board
www.perthshire.co.uk/ – consumer site

Perthshire Tourist Board – business to business site
www.perthshireexchange.net/

Scottish Borders Tourist Board – consumer site
www.scot-borders.co.uk

Shetland Islands Tourist Board – consumer site
www.shetland-tourism.co.uk/

VisitScotland
23 Ravelston Terrace
Edinburgh EH4 3TP
Tel: (0131) 332 2433
www.scotexchange.net

WALES
Mid Wales Tourism – consumer site
www.mid-wales-tourism.org.uk

North Wales Tourism – consumer site
www.nwt.co.uk/

Southern Wales – consumer site
www.southandwestwales.roomcheck.co.uk

Visit Wales
Welsh Assembly Government
Brunel House
2 Fitzalan Road
Cardiff CF24 0UY
Tel: (029) 2049 9909
Fax: (029) 2048 5031

IRELAND
Belfast
Bord Fáilte
53 Castle Street
Belfast BT1 1GH

Tel: (00) 44 28 9032 7888
Fax: (00) 44 28 9024 0201

Belfast Visitor and Convention Bureau
47 Donegal Place
Belfast BT1 5AD
Tel: (028) 9024 5829
Fax: (028) 9024 5829
www.gotobelfast.com

Bord Fáilte,
Baggot Street Bridge
Baggot Street
Dublin 2
Tel: (00) 353 1602 4000
Fax: (00) 353 1602 4100

Causeway Coast and Glens Ltd
11 Lodge Road
Coleraine
Co. Londonderry BT52 1LU
Tel: (028) 7032 7720
Fax: (028) 7032 7719
www.causewaycoastandglens.com

Derry Visitor and Convention Bureau
44 Foyle Street
Derry BT48 6AT
Tel: (028) 7137 7577
www.derryvisitor.com

Dublin Tourism Centre
Suffolk Street
Dublin 2
www.visitdublin.com

Fermanagh Lakeland Tourism
Wellington Road
Enniskillen
Co. Fermanagh BT74 7EF
Tel: (028) 6634 6736
Fax: (028) 6632 5511

Kingdoms of Down
40 West Street
Newtownards BT23 4EN
Tel: (028) 9182 2881
Fax: (028) 9182 2202
www.kingdomsofdown.com

Northern Ireland Tourist Board
St Anne's Court
59 North Street
Belfast BT1 1NB
Tel: (028) 9023 1221
Fax: (028) 9024 0960
www.nitb.com

South East Tourism (Carlow, Kilkenny, South Tipperary, Waterford and Wexford)
41 The Quay
Waterford
Ireland
Tel: +353 51 875823
Fax: +353 51 877388
www.southeastireland.com

ISLE OF MAN
Department of Tourism and Leisure
Sea Terminal
Douglas
Isle of Man IM1 2RG
Tel: 01624 68680
Fax: 01624 68680
Email: tourism@gov.im

CHANNEL ISLANDS
Jersey Tourism
Liberation Square
St. Helier JE1 1BB
Tel: (01534) 500702

BED & BREAKFAST AND FARMSTAY ASSOCIATIONS

Ireland
Bed and Breakfast Association Northern Ireland
Aisling House
7 Taunton Avenue
Belfast
Northern Ireland BT 15 4AD
Tel: (028) 9077 1529

Bed and Breakfast Ireland
Belle Ek Road
Ballyshannon
Co. Donegal
Tel: (072) 51377

Irish Farm Holidays Association
Head Office
2 Michael Street
Limerick
Tel: (061) 400700

Northern Ireland Farm and Country Holidays Association
Greenmount Lodge
Greenmount Road
Omagh
County Tyrone
Northern Ireland BT 79 OYE
Tel: (028) 8284 1325
Fax: (028) 8284 0019
Email: greenmountlodge@lineone.net
www.nifcha.com

England
The Bed & Breakfast and Homestay Association
103 Dawes Road
London SW6 7DU
Tel: (020) 7385 9922
Fax: (020) 7385 7575
Email: info@bbha.org.uk

The Bed and Breakfast Association
c/o The Pheasants B&B
24 Greenhill
Sherborne
Dorset DT9 4EW
Tel: (01935) 815252
Fax: (01935) 812938
www.BandBassociation.org

Farm Stay UK
C/o Farm Stay UK Ltd
National Agricultural Centre
Stoneleigh Park
Warwickshire CV8 2LZ
Tel: (024) 7669 6909
Fax: (024) 7669 6630

B&B listing agencies
Academy Travel
PO Box 645
London SW16 4SG
Tel: (020) 8679 5738
Fax: (020) 8679 1798
Location of properties: All UK

Always Welcome Homes
11 Westerdale Road
Greenwich
London SE10 0LW
Tel: (020) 8858 0821
Fax: (020) 8858 7743
Location of properties: All UK

At Home in London
70 Black Lion Lane
London W6 9BE
Tel: (020) 8748 1943
Fax: (020) 8748 2701
Location of properties: London

Avalon Student Travel
11 Marlborough Place
Brighton BN1 1UB
Tel: (01273) 243395
Fax: (01273) 243396
Location of properties: All UK

B&B My Guest
103 Dawes Road
London SW6 7DU
Tel: (0870) 444 3840
Fax: (0870) 444 3841
www.beduk.co.uk
Location of properties: All UK

Bed & Breakfast (GB)
94–96 Bell Street
Henley-on-Thames
Oxfordshire RG9 1XS
Tel: (01491) 578803
Fax: (01491) 410806
www.bedbreak.com
Location of properties: UK

Bed and Breakfast Nationwide
PO Box 2100
Clacton on Sea
Essex CO16 9BW
Tel: (01255) 831235
Fax: (01255) 831437
www.bedandbreakfastnationwide.com
Location of properties: UK and Ireland

The Brackett Agency
Brockhillburn
Ettrickbridge
Selkirk TD7 5JH
Tel: (01750) 52210
Fax: (01750) 52210
Location of properties: Edinburgh

Centa UK Ltd
Foresters
31 Chapel Street
Cam
Dursley
Gloucester GL11 5NY
Tel: (01453) 548200/(01453) 549996
Fax: (01453) 548200
www.centauk.co.uk
Location of properties: Cotswolds, Yorkshire Dales and Moors

Distinctly Different
Bradford Old Windmill
4 Masons Lane
Bradford-on-Avon
Wiltshire BA15 1QN
Tel: (01225) 866648
Fax: (01225) 866648
Location of properties: England, Wales and Scotland

En Famille Agency (Britain)
Suite 16
Gerrard House Business Centre
Worthing Road
East Preston
West Sussex BN16 1AW
Tel: (01903) 783636
Fax: (01903) 783630
Location of properties: All Britain

English Host Holidays
21 Manor Way
Hayling Island
Hampshire PO11 9JH
Tel: (01705) 46219
Fax: (01705) 468227
Location of properties: Southern England

Euro-Academy Ltd
77a George Street
Croydon
Surrey CR0 1LD
Tel: (020) 8681 2905
Fax: (020) 8681 8850
Location of properties: All UK

Euroyouth Ltd
301 Westborough Road
Southend-on-Sea (Westcliff)
Essex SS0 9PT
Tel: (01702) 341434
Fax: (01702) 330104
Location of properties: Mostly Southend-on-Sea, some London suburbs

Families in Britain
Martins Cottage, Martins Lane
Birdham
Chichester
Sussex PO20 7AU
Tel: (01243) 512222
Fax: (01243) 511377
Location of properties: UK

Farm Stay UK (formerly the Farm Holiday Bureau)
National Agriculture Centre
Stoneleigh Park
Warwickshire CV8 2LZ
Tel: (02476) 696909
Fax: (02476) 696630
www.farmstayuk.co.uk
Location of properties: UK and Northern Ireland

Festival Beds
38 Moray Place
Edinburgh EH3 6BT
Tel: (0131) 225 1101
Fax: (0131) 623 7123
Location of properties: Edinburgh city centre

FERN (Franco European Relations Negotiators)
105 Gordon Road
Camberley
Surrey GU15 2JQ
Tel: (01276) 27033
Fax: (01276) 27033
Location of properties: Outer London, Surrey, Hampshire, Berkshire

Happy Homes
Beaufort Street
Chelsea
London SW3
Tel: (020) 7352 5121
Fax: (020) 7352 5121
www.happy-homes.com
Location of properties: Mainly central London, especially south-west

Holiday Hosts
59 Cromwell Road
London SW19 8LF
Tel: (020) 8540 7942
Fax: (020) 8540 2827
Location of properties: South and west London

Home from Home Accommodation Service
The Old Granary
Fillongley
Nr Coventry CV7 8PB
Tel: (01676) 541896
Fax: (01203) 256825
Location of properties: England

Homes Away
3 Aldham Hall
New Wanstead
London E11 2SQ
Tel: (020) 8530 2271
Fax: (020) 8530 2271
Location of properties: Quiet residential areas. Woodford, South
Woodford, Wanstead and east London

Host and Guest Service
103 Dawes Road
London SW6 7DU
Tel: (020) 7385 9922
Fax: (020) 7386 7575
www.host-guest.co.uk
Location of properties: UK, especially London

Jolaine Agency
18 Escot Way
Barnet
Hertfordshire EN5 3AN
Tel: (020) 8449 1334
Fax: (020) 8449 9183
Location of properties: Mainly north-west London suburbs – other areas on request

Knights in Britain
Arundell House
High Street
Tisbury
Wiltshire SP3 6PS
Tel: (01747) 871221
Fax: (01747) 871281
Location of properties: All UK

The London Bed & Breakfast Agency Limited
71 Fellows Road
London NW3 3JY
Tel: (020) 7586 2768
Fax: (020) 7586 6567
Location of properties: North, south, south-west and west London

London First Choice Accommodation
111 Hill Rise
Greenford UB6 8PE
Tel: (020) 8575 8877
Fax: (020) 8575 8877
Location of properties: Central London and suburbs

London Homestead Services
Coombe Wood Road
Kingston Upon Thames
Surrey KT2 7JY
Tel: (020) 8949 4455
Fax: (020) 8549 5492
Location of properties: London

Mondial Agency
32 Links Road
West Wickham
Kent BR4 0QW
Tel: (020) 8777 6271
Fax: (020) 8777 6765
Location of properties: UK

New East International Ltd
PO Box 292
Pinner HA5 1UF
Tel: (020) 8933 1460
Fax: (020) 8866 5520
Location of properties: UK

Norfolk and Suffolk Farm Holiday Group
Monterey
Lodge Close
Thurston
Bury St Edmunds
Suffolk IP31 3RS
Tel/Fax: (01359) 231013
www.farmstayanglia.co.uk
Location of properties: Norfolk and Suffolk

Overseas Visitor Service (OVS)
192 Brighton Road
Lancing
West Sussex BN15 8LJ
Tel: (01903) 762097
Fax: (01273) 453143
Location of properties: Lancing and Worthing, West Sussex

Peaceful Holidays Ltd
97 Fieldhead Rd
Guiseley
Leeds LS20 8DU
Tel: (01943) 872765
Fax: (01973) 872765
Location of properties: Yorkshire Dales and Moors

The Primrose Hill Agency for Bed and Breakfast
14 Edis Street
London NW1 8LG
Tel: (020) 7722 6869
Fax: (020) 7916 2240
Location of properties: North London – Hampstead, Highgate,
Primrose Hill

Thameside Homestay
120 Thurleston Avenue
Morden
Surrey SM4 4EG
Tel: (020) 8395 0389
Fax: (020) 8395 0389
Location of properties: All UK

Uptown Reservations
50 Christchurch Street
Chelsea
London SW3 4AR
Tel: (020) 7351 3445
Fax: (020) 7351 9383
Location of properties: Kensington, Chelsea, Knightsbridge, Belgravia,
Holland Park, Parsons Green, Notting Hill

Welcome Homes and Hotels
21 Kellerton Road
London SE13 5RB
Tel: (020) 8265 1212
Fax: (020) 8852 3243
www.welcomehomes.co.uk
Location of properties: All UK

Wolsey Lodges
9 Market Place
Hadleigh
Ipswich
Suffolk IP7 5DL
Tel: (01473) 822058
Fax: (01473) 827444
www.wolsey-lodges.co.uk
Location of properties: All UK

LIQUOR LICENCES

Here are the contact details of two legal firms who can assist you in securing the appropriate liquor licence for your establishment.

William Fry, Solicitors
Fitzwilton House
Wilton Place
Dublin 2
Ireland
Tel: +353 1 639 5000
Fax: +353 1 639 5333
www.williamfry.ie/licensinglaw.html

Fisher Jones Greenwood
Norfolk House, Southway
Colchester
Essex CO2 7BA
Tel: (01206) 578282
Fax: (01206) 760282
www.lawcentre.co.uk

ENERGY EFFICIENCY

There are many Energy Efficiency Advice Centres (EEACs) across the UK who give advice to people in their locality. We suggest you call the national EEAC free-phone number 0800 512 012.

You may also wish to contact the Carbon Trust, a sister organisation by clicking onto www.thecarbontrust.co.uk

BUSINESS NAME REGISTRATION

For businesses in England or Wales
Business Names Section
Companies House
Crown Way
Cardiff CF14 3UZ
Tel: (029) 2038 0362

For businesses in Scotland
The Registrar of Companies
Companies House
37 Castle Terrace
Edinburgh EH1 2EB
Tel: (0131) 535 5800

For businesses in the Republic of Ireland
Companies Registration Office
Parnell House
14 Parnell Square
Ireland
Dublin 1
Tel: (01) 804 5200

For businesses in Northern Ireland
Companies Registry
64 Chichester Street
Belfast BTI 4JX
Tel: (028) 9054 4888/4999

BED SUPPLIER
Sealy United Kingdom
Station Road
Aspatria
Carlisle
Cumbria CA5 2AS
Tel: (016973) 20342 for both the UK and Ireland.

HOME RENOVATION INTERNET SITE
The following is a helpful Internet site on house renovation tips and
ideas: www.thisoldhouse.com

Index